ADULT BELIEVERS

Peter Ball

ADULT BELIEVING

A Guide to the Christian Initiation of Adults

Peter Ball

PAULIST PRESS
NEW YORK & MAHWAH

First published 1988
by A.R. Mowbray & Co. Ltd,
Saint Thomas House, Becket Street,
Oxford, OX1 1SJ

Library of Congress Cataloging-in-Publication Data

Ball, Peter.
    Adult, believing.

    Bibliography: p.
    1. Church membership. 2. Christian education of adults. 3. Catechumens. 4. Initiation rites—Religious aspects—Christianity. 5. Christian life—Anglican authors. I. Title.
    BV820.B35   1988   268'.434   88-25474
    ISBN 0-8091-3053-X (pbk.)

Published by Paulist Press
997 Macarthur Blvd.
Mahwah, N.J. 07430

Printed and bound in the United States of America

Contents

Preface

This book is written to be read by clergy and lay people who are concerned with the Church's ministry of presenting the Gospel as an adult faith for adults. In the first place it is meant to help them to develop appropriate ways of accompanying men and women towards Christian faith and commitment in preparation for baptism, confirmation and life as a communicant within the Church. I hope it may stimulate both action and reaction. Action, in that people will be encouraged to undertake what is for them a new and fuller way of working with enquirers and candidates for Christian initiation. Reaction, in that people who are either excited or dismayed by what happens as a result, will respond to me and take part with a growing number of men and women who are trying to meet the questions and the needs which newcomers present to the Church in a serious and open way.

Most of what follows is about the early stages of the journey of faith, though Christians further along their journey may find it good to be reminded of the importance of their own first steps. There are also some parts which will be useful as guides for church members of some experience who recognize that they are called to deeper understanding of their faith and to deeper commitment to its implications in their lives.

There is nothing secret about all this and enquirers about the faith and the life of the Christian church are welcome to read my book and judge whether it could be for them. What really matters, though, is meeting and talking with the local Christian community. Books can only go so far; they can describe, but they can't live.

Acknowledgements

I make no claims that the material to be found in these pages is original. Over the years I have learned a great deal from many people, professional and lay, in the field of helping adults into faith. In particular I recognize the influence of the Adult Catechumenate in France and other countries on the continent of Europe and mention especially the help of Henri Bourgeois and Gérard Reniers. In Britain, apart from all I have learned in association with people at St. Nicholas, Shepperton, I recognize a debt to the Roman Catholics working with the Rite of Christian Initiation of Adults in England, not least among them to Patrick Purnell, Céline Murphy and Michael Fewell. Several Americans have helped a great deal, in particular James Dunning, Karen Hinman Powell, John Westerhoff and James Fowler. No doubt all these people will recognize their ideas and their influence in what I have written, but I have to bear full responsibility for the whole. They are not to blame for errors and omissions!

I thank the authors and publishers who have given permission for extended quotation from their work. The details of the books and other publications are in the Notes.

1

Introducing the Themes

I start from the conviction that Christianity is an adult religion for adults. Even deciding to follow the direction of Jesus that we should become like little children to enter the Kingdom takes a mature decision. He was a fully grown man when he taught, ministered and was crucified. We know his close companions were adult men and women and certainly the proclamation of the Gospel by the first church preachers brought about the conversion of mature people.

It is clear from the statistics of people confirmed in the Church of England that adults still respond. Indeed the proportion of adults to teenagers grows steadily, as does their actual number. What has perhaps not changed is the way in which they are prepared for Christian initiation. Much work has been done to develop the approaches and methods of adult education in the secular world. Some of the new thinking is now affecting the Church. Alongside this there has been a shift in attitudes among Christians, most notably in the Roman Catholic Church since the Second Vatican Council. This shift, which has slightly different expressions in different denominations, is seen in liturgical revision, in changed expectations of the ministry of lay and ordained people, and in a new (or renewed) awareness of the role of Christian communities in the mission of the Gospel to the world.

Within this range of movements is the renewal of a way to prepare men and women for the sacraments of baptism, confirmation and the eucharist which has come to be known as the Adult Catechumenate or Rite of Christian Initiation of Adults. (There is a note about the language, including the word 'Catechumenate' on page 6). It offers an alternative

1

outline for what has been known for a long time as 'The Adult Confirmation Class'.

The background from which I write is that of the Rector of the Parish of St. Nicholas, Shepperton and more recently as a Canon at St. Paul's Cathedral. This means that I write as an Anglican from an Anglican base, but for nearly twenty years I have been involved in close co-operation with members of other churches in the work of adult initiation. In particular I have been an active member of the European Conference on the Adult Catechumenate and worked closely with the North American Forum on the Catechumenate. So, although most of this book is couched in the language and practice of the Church of England, it is based on the conviction that the adult journey into Christian faith and commitment is not a denominational matter. I hope that readers who are not Anglicans will be able to translate easily enough into their own language where necessary.

Marion's Story

'Since childhood I'd wanted to get to know the mysterious person you never see but who understands everything, is concerned about everything and who above all loves everything and everyone. When I grew up I trained as a nurse and found that the faith of sick people affected me deeply. Like everyone else I had my troubles and upsets but I recognize that these were leading me towards my Creator. Then, when my baby Andrew was born, I decided to ask to join the Church. I felt I needed help in bringing him up the right way.

'I was in a group with the Curate, Barbara, Stephen and Gillian who were church members. We had deep discussions on many subjects; human life, God who made us, all that Jesus did for us. What stood out for me was how open I could be, thanks to the welcome which made me feel at home. Living through the course was like being born again, starting all over again – a kind of apprenticeship leading to meeting with Jesus Christ. His teaching is a wonderful school.

'Although nothing much seems to have altered – my life is

just the same – there are all different vibes inside me. It's as though by preparing to be baptized, I've started a whole new adventure. I've found a new life, very strange but truly pointing towards God and towards other people through Jesus.

'I'd like to add my very warm thanks to all the people who have helped me to know Jesus. Some of them have done it consciously and some without ever realising it.'

The person I have in mind as I write is the man or woman, ordained or lay, who has accepted the responsibility of acting as guide to someone like Marion on their journey from unbelief or little belief in Jesus to that point where they can make their profession of faith and be baptized or confirmed and accept their call to be a Christian in the Church. My book is not meant as a detailed how-to-do-it guide like a car owner's workshop manual. It gives some answers but certainly suggests no techniques which are guaranteed universally successful. Rather it is a base on which people can build their own way of working. What I hope for is that a group of people in a Church community will with their clergy work together to see how best the Church in their place is to fulfil the injunction of Jesus, 'Go forth therefore and make all nations my disciples; baptize people everywhere in the name of the Father and the Son and the Holy Spirit, and teach them to observe all that I have commanded you'. (Matt. 28.19f).

There's a powerful note in the Introduction to the Roman Catholic *Rite of Christian Initiation of Adults* which expresses that Gospel spirit of mission which I hope underlies all this book stands for:

The people of God, as represented by the local Church, should understand and show by their concern that the initiation of adults is the responsibility of all the baptized. Therefore the community must always be fully prepared in the pursuit of its apostolic vocation to give help to those who are searching for Christ. In the various circumstances of daily life, even as in the apostolate, all the followers of Christ have the obligation of spreading the faith according to their abilities.[1]

The Roots

The idea of the adult catechumenate, as it is expressed in the
Rite of Christian Initiation of Adults and similar Rites in
churches like the Episcopal Church of the U.S.A. and the
Anglican Church in South Africa, has its roots in the church
of the first three centuries after Jesus. Until the Christian
religion became established in the Roman Empire under the
Emperor Constantine with his edict of Milan in 313AD, the
Christian community was for much of its life a persecuted
minority. Membership was something both valuable and
dangerous. It mattered a great deal that enquirers and con-
verts should be carefully prepared and also carefully ex-
amined before they were admitted to the fellowship. It would
have been important to make sure that they were not police
spies. On the other hand it was only right that if they were
liable to be arrested themselves and brought to court for their
Christian allegiance, they should be well aware of the commitment they were making. This resulted in the development
of a preparation lasting two or three years for those under
instruction before they came to be baptized.

Recent years have seen the principles that lay behind the
early Church's catechumenate re-expressed in many parts of
the world where the church is in mission to a non-christian
society.

For people to whom the whole concept is new I have
written a summary of what the modern adult catechumenate
is at the end of this chapter. It is easily skipped by those who
already have experienced it.

Help Needed

It is to help people who are involved in the task of accompanying enquirers along their road to baptism that I am
writing this book. There are many different ways in which
you can help someone else to know Jesus. I suspect that our
trouble in the Church of England (and Anglicans are by no

means alone in this!) is that we have tended to become one-sided in our attitudes of instruction. We look to books and to courses which emphasize the need to understand. We explain Christian doctrine. Manuals for adult confirmation classes tend to be designed like simplified courses for students in theology. Of course there is more to it than that, but with this as the general approach it is natural that the main (often the only) person responsible for the preparation should be the person who has had that sort of theological education.

I am pleading for balance to be restored and for much more weight to be given to individuals with the questions and the experience they bring. I am pleading for much more weight to be given to those other aspects of what it means to be human. Certainly intellectual understanding is important. But we also need to work with our awareness; our feelings; our artistic imaginations, perceptions and creativity; our relationships and our belonging to a community. With all that we, of course, need to enter into the whole realm of what we call the spiritual.

To set out to work in this way from experience rather than from a laid out pattern of doctrinal beliefs can be frightening for some people, even threatening. But I believe it is more in accord with the truth of most people's spiritual journey than leading from the head. In everyday life we experience first; then we reflect upon our experience to make sense of it for ourselves. We do not start with an analysis and then have experiences to fit in with that!

From this approach follow two suggestions. The first is that it is often a handicap to rely on a previous theological education, unless of course it has been so worked into and through that it is part and parcel of personal experience. Often the person who has reflected deeply (and theologically) on their own experience of life and community and the world is a better guide for an enquirer than a person who has spent years in the study of the doctrines of the Church. The second is that this thinking, reflective but not 'theologically educated' Christian is, in today's Church climate, going to feel that they are quite inadequate to the task of guiding anyone else to Christ because they 'don't know enough'. It is one of my intentions in this book to help that person to see it is not a question of being ashamed of the knowledge they do not have. It is a matter of being reassured and confident in those real gifts with which God has endowed them in order to share them with others. There is strong encouragement to move away from syllabus-based instruction in the direction of the journey accompanying the enquirer along the road of conversion. This, as we shall see, involves change in all aspects of a man's or woman's life and personality. Conversion concerns their attitudes, their understanding and knowledge, their spirituality and their relationships and moral choices.

Language

One of the difficulties anyone has in trying to write or speak about the catechumenate is the words. Many of the terms used come directly from the first centuries of the Church and are Greek or Latin. This means that anyone coming new to the subject is likely to be confused or put off by being faced with a new language, even though the topics, activities and relationships are really very straightforward and easy to enter into. The trouble is that, once you have learned the special words, it is so much quicker and easier to use them – despite the dangers of upsetting other people. I have tried to keep their use to a minimum, but some are inescapable, like 'catechumenate' itself.

The family of words beginning 'catech-' comes from the Greek and has the common thread of teaching or instructing, especially in the specific sense of giving instruction to people preparing for baptism. The name for a person being instructed is 'catechumen' and the process of instructing someone in the faith is 'catechesis'. A catechism is a summary of a church's teaching and catechetics is the study of how the teaching is done. (This book is an exercise in catechetics.)

The main advantage of using this cluster of words is that it avoids long phrases about 'people who are in the process of preparing for baptism' if you simply call them 'catechumens'. But I generally prefer the extra words for the sake of avoiding unnecessary mystification. Other authors and trainers in the catechumenate are prepared to expect people to learn a new glossary of words to accompany a new outlook on the whole scene of initiation.

The Outline

The plan of the book is as follows. Chapter 2 is about the journey taken by someone towards Christian faith, commitment and initiation into the Church. It enters into some of the consequences of thinking in terms of personal journey rather than dogmatic syllabus.

Chapter 3 is about what is taught and learned. In technical terms it is about catechesis for adults, how people learn and mature in coming to Christian faith and how those already in the Church can help them. It includes suggested ways of developing the dialogue between people's lives and the gospel, which for me is the main task of theology.

Chapter 4 is largely about praying. Its purpose is to provide the Christian companion with a brief survey of the ways people can find and express their friendship with God so that they can have some confidence in talking openly about spirituality.

Chapter 5 enters into the topic of conversion and tries to show both the vital importance of change in the catechumenal journey and the many varied ways in which it takes place.

In Chapter 6 the idea of conversion is brought forward to include the new Christian's part in the Church's mission to and ministry in the world.

Practical suggestions about the training and support of leaders in the different ministries of the Catechumenate come in Chapter 7. An Appendix of books and other resource material and groups closes the book.

A NOTE

What is the Catechumenate?

It depends which part of the world you live in and what
Church you belong to whether you talk about *The Rite of
Christian Initiation* (*R.C.I.A.* for short) or *The Catechumenate* (or perhaps *The Adult Catechumenate*). The titles refer to
exactly the same thing. There is a stream of experience over
fifty years of Christian missions in Africa and elsewhere and
of the work of the Church in France and other countries in
Europe and French-speaking Canada. This stream tends to
talk of 'the Catechumenate'. Following the directive of the
Second Vatican Council the Roman Catholic Church produced the official *Rite of Christian Initiation of Adults*, first
published in English in 1976. Roman Catholics in Britain, for
example, speak regularly of *The R.C.I.A.* Anglicans in South
Africa and the U.S.A. have also produced texts along the same
lines for the admission to a period of preparation beforehand
of people asking for baptism.

The Catechumenate—R.C.I.A., marks a distinct change
from the past in the way people are prepared for initiation. It
involves a new set of attitudes on the part of the Christian
community; it introduces new ministries for people in the
Church and it presents a series of liturgical events in which the
Church and the new Christians celebrate the stages of their
journey into faith.

The Main Points

It will be helpful for people who are new to the idea of the
catechumenate if I outline the key notes.

WELCOME

The way in which the Church and its members and ministers
receive an enquirer is of the very greatest importance.
Warmth matters. Respect matters. Acceptance matters. These

aspects of welcome are vital at the start of anyone's journey towards a commitment to Christ within his Church. Clergy and people need continually to be aware of this and to review how they behave. People notice how the vicarage phone is answered, whether there is a smile at the church door for people venturing in for the first time to hear their Banns of Marriage read, or what kind of response is given to a request to have their new baby christened.

Welcome is extended to people as they are and for what they are. Many, perhaps virtually all, churches have some sort of preconditions they consciously or unconsciously put as turnstiles at the entrance. One of the most damning remarks is 'They're not the kind of people you'd expect to come to church'. Behind it lie all kinds of expectations, social class, dress, age or personal behaviour. Few congregations are free of them. What is needed is an openness and a valuing of people with all they bring with them. The example we need to follow is in the ministry of Jesus described in the Gospels.

Lay men and women are often more likely to be effective welcomers than the clergy. After all they are not paid to be nice to people! In the catechumenate it is lay members of the Church who have the prime responsibility of acting as sponsors, welcoming friends and guides to new people.

FAITH-SHARING

At the heart of the catechumenate is a person's conversion to a living, committed faith in Jesus Christ; expressed in a life guided by his teaching and in active membership of his Church. One of the routes to this is through open sharing of belief between the Christian friend and the enquirer.

This is a two-way process and, again, involves that respect for the enquirer and his or her faith which is part of welcome. People begin where they are and where they are needs to be celebrated as true for them. They need to express their own faith whatever it may be and however inadequate the Christian may feel it is. The dialogue has to be a genuine meeting of two people, not a cloak for indoctrination.

Later in the book there is a chapter on the content and
possible methods of this faith-sharing. Suffice it here to say
that although head knowledge of the Christian faith is an
important part of faith, far more important is to help people
into a personal awareness of God and to accompany them
through the stages of their own experience of conversion.

AN ACCOMPANIED JOURNEY

The language used in the catechumenate is often journey
language. It is about movement and change of direction. It is
also about travelling companions.

The journey is one which is personal to the individual.
There are recognized stages which most people go through,
but speeds vary, strengths and weaknesses vary, and perhaps
most significant, length of time varies.

Notice that generally in the catechumenate the duration of
a person's journey from start to baptism or confirmation is
considerably longer than is often reckoned to be needed in
'Adult Instruction Classes'. A year is normal, eighteen months
nothing unusual. This is because what is at issue is not
whether the candidate has attended all the items in the course
of church teaching, but whether he has matured as a Christian to that point where baptism is appropriate, whether he
shows signs of the changes in life which are evidence of a
personal conversion to faith in Christ. These things are to do
with development, a kind of organic or dynamic change and
growth which of their nature take their own time and need to
be given that time. The measure of the catechumenate is not
the syllabus nor the calendar – nor even the priest's need for a
successful new member rate! – but the truth of the candidate's
journey.

They do not take the journey alone. They have as companions and guides members of the Christian community. Sponsors, catechists, leaders, friends and guides, however they are
described, have the ministry of welcoming, sharing faith,
pastoring, instructing and helping the enquirer on the journey. The image is of a coach rather than a teacher, someone

who runs alongside an athlete, a guide who shares knowledge of a route they have travelled already, who journeys with a newcomer.

Journeys pass landmarks and the catechumenate journey has certain recognized stages which are marked by celebration. These are the Rites of the R.C.I.A. Here let me emphasize that there is far, far more to the R.C.I.A. than a series of good, interesting and impressive services. The Rites or Liturgies which celebrate the stages along the journey are effective signs of what is happening spiritually and personally to the people who are on their way. They are signs to them and to the congregation of what it means to become a Christian.

There is first a time of enquiry, the 'Pre-catechumenate', during which someone meets the church, tests out what it has to say to them; whether the people are friendly or not; if it is worth persevering with. It is a time of initial encounter, of getting to know, of telling and listening to stories.

Those who want to go further express this desire at the celebration of Entry into the Catechumenate or Admission of Catechumens, in which they are formally welcomed by the congregation and signed with the cross as people who have made their first step into the household of faith.

There follows the time of learning, growing and maturing which is the period of the catechumenate proper. It takes as long as it needs. General experience seems to point to an average time of nine to twelve months.

At the close of this period comes the Call of the people to be baptized. In the classic pattern Easter is the time for initiation at the Vigil and the Solemn Call (The Rite of Election or the Rite of Inscription or Enrolling of Names) takes place at the beginning of Lent. At it the Church in the person of the Bishop or his nominee examines the people who are to be baptized, calls them to prepare for their baptism and invites them to sign their names on the roll of those so called. The people who have accompanied them and the whole congregation are responsible for sponsoring them and giving evidence of their fitness for the Sacrament.

Lent or the equivalent period leading up to the Baptism is the time of Enlightenment, a spiritual preparation, often marked by special celebrations of prayer (the Scrutinies) and the symbolic presentations to the candidates of the Creed and the Lord's Prayer.

The centre of the whole journey is, of course, the Celebration of Baptism, Confirmation and the Eucharist, at which the whole congregation should celebrate the entry of new brothers and sisters into the death and new life of the Risen Christ.

There follows (again classically from Easter to Pentecost) the time of Mystagogia when the newly baptised enter into the meaning of the sacrament and have the chance to witness to the congregation of what has happened to them.

Evidence from many parts of the world and from people of different churches and cultures shows how much value has been found in the liturgical expression of these turning points. Candidates have spoken of the strengthening they have received and members of congregations have been moved to reflect deeply on what their own Christian commitment means for them.

CHRISTIAN COMMUNITY

'In the catechumenate we don't talk about Church; we make Church.' The aim is to provide an opportunity for the enquirer to experience what it means to be part of a community where the love of God is expressed by love of the neighbour. To this end in this book I propose the basic unit of the catechumenate is a group of about ten people where this experience of life in the Body of Christ is possible. The life of the whole congregation is too large and a one-to-one relationship of enquirer and catechist or priest too restricted. What is needed is a human-scale group where it is possible to know and be known; to be accepted and learn to forgive; to pray together and to support and be supported by one another.

In another sense the catechumenate is essentially concerned

with Christian community. It is the work of the whole community, people and priest together. Each baptized member of the Church has a ministry in it. Some have the ministry of intercession, of participation in the liturgical celebration, of being the welcoming, supporting community. Others have more specific roles as sponsors and catechists, or as spiritual directors and helpers, or again as leaders and trainers of leaders.

In an age where 'every member ministry' is a catchphrase in many parts of the Church, the Catechumenate is a field where the phrase finds 'lively' practical expression which seems to put it into effect in a natural and proper way.

2

A Journey Shared

Essential Topics

Language reflects attitudes and beliefs. In this book my beliefs
about what is important for the man or woman coming to the
Christian faith, personal commitment and initiation into the
Church are reflected by the use of language to do with
journeying, with growth into maturity and with search. I am
writing about a process which is concerned to help someone
discover and become what God has it in his plan for them to
be. This concerns the whole of a person. It affects their
understanding, their attitudes, their spirituality, their relationships with other people and the choices they make in life.
It is affected by their character, by their experience of living
from birth to the present day, by their friends and by the
society and communities to which they belong. I aim to
present a holistic approach to the work of adult catechesis. It
is something very wide, as wide as life itself.

Journeys always have to begin somewhere. It is important
that people responsible for accompanying others recognize
where their starting point is. Begin where they are. My own
experience in common, I suspect, with most other Church
leaders in parishes and chaplaincies is that by far the greatest
number of people who come to us for baptism or confirmation or for help in their search for a meaning in life have at
some time previously come into contact with Christianity in
some way.

I write in the second half of the 1980s. It may well be that
the movement of Britain away from organized Christianity

and from exposure to Christian teaching and influence will accelerate. It may mean that in a relatively short time there will be fewer and fewer people who will have received even a nominal amount of Christian education or contact with the Church. Even today there will, of course, be people who begin with no understanding from their past about Christianity and there will be people from other faiths. But most will have some idea of their own what Christianity is about.

Faith

The journey is about faith. John Shea has a telling remark: 'The right question is not, "Do you have faith?", but, "What is your faith?" '[1] The point where people start their journey is in fact a point of faith, their own faith. Even if it is not what is generally recognized as religious, there is something in everyone which gives them (or fails to give them) a sense of purpose or meaning or simply a sense of who they are. It is their attitude towards life, how they lean into life.

Faith in this sense may seem a much reduced idea to someone who is used to talking about the Christian Faith. It can be both a strong, positive, creative attitude to life or an empty, negative and painful attitude. There is no need here to go into the psychological explanations of how we come by the sort of personalities we have. It is enough simply to ask you to think about, say, six people you know, the first six or so who come to mind, and to ask yourself what you know about their faith, what, deep down is important to them. The possibilities are infinite. Among them you may well recognise the importance of family with the loving or less than loving relationship of parents and children; the sense of being given worth by someone who loves you; a pride in skills and achievements, your own or those of someone you admire – 'My dad was regimental heavyweight champion'. There are people whose lives seem to be governed by status or money and people who have almost given up making choices in life because of a kind of apathy which sees everything as 'Fate'.

The faith, in this wide sense, which has brought someone towards the Church may well be one of questioning. People become dissatisfied with attitudes which no longer meet their needs. Something may have happened in their life to cause them to reassess the principles by which they live.

That is a rather analytical way of describing the sort of thing which happens to a young man when his wife gives birth to their first baby, or to a middle-aged woman when the mother she has nursed through her long final illness at last dies. Or the kind of challenges to making sense of life that are presented by unemployment to the school-leaver in a derelict steel town, or to the car worker whose settled habits of regular work are shattered by the closure of the factory. Questions about who I am, where I am going and why, are raised in a fresh way and with a different urgency.

What adult catechesis is concerned with is recognizing those questions and accepting their importance for this woman or that man. Christians who are accompanying enquirers will want to help them to understand their own questions and will work with them to see what answers are to be found in all that comes under the label of Christianity. In Chapter 3 I shall be looking in more detail at ways in which this can be done. For the moment let me simply say that the task is to help forward growth, change and development. It is the movement from the faith which the enquirer brings towards a mature Christian faith. Catechesis of this kind takes the person seriously; it listens to and respects the story of their life; it presents to them the story of God's love and helps them to meet the challenge of God's story to their own.

Choices

The use of 'journey language' implies that real choices are there to be made and that the choices belong to the person making the journey. The responses to God's challenge and initiative can only be made by them. They will be lived out in changes made in real life. It is the whole man or the whole woman we are dealing with and they have the right to expect that the Church should respect their God-given adulthood and humanity.

Sooner or later the question of conscience will come up. Right and wrong are important to everyone, though not everyone will have the same judgement on what is right and what is wrong. For many Christianity is really about good behaviour, living by 'Christian Principles', 'following the Sermon on the Mount' – or even simply 'not doing anyone any harm'. Part of the work of the journey towards Christian maturity is the working out in practical terms what these 'Christian Principles' are and how they are to be applied in everyday life.

Journey language also implies that there are by no means always easy answers, nor is there any guarantee of success – whatever 'success' may mean in this enterprise. Certainly there are some people whose way into Christian belief and whose life as Christians look easy and happily God-given. For others the journey is harder; it calls for patience and an understanding of yourself and of other people. As falling in love is a painful process for some individuals, so can conversion be.

Accompanying

The other aspect of journey language is that it carries with it the image of companions sharing the journey, rather than the image of teachers passing on information. This accompanying is essential. The Christian community as a whole is responsible for the welcome and nurture of enquirers and new Christians. The duty is primarily discharged by those who have immediate contact with them, their friends and sponsors and their catechists, the people who are charged with their formation as Christians, whether they are professional ministers and clergy or, more probably, lay people.

Later in the book I deal with ways of training and continuing help for the people who are responsible. Sufficient at this point to say the best way to learn how to accompany others on a journey of faith is to enter yourself into the experience of being open about your own faith with someone else. It is worth quoting James Dunning's maxim, 'Thou shalt not do unto others What thou hast not done for thyself'.

What I hope you will do as you read this book is check out what I write or suggest by talking it through with a friend. Make time to discuss at quite a deep level the things that really matter to you. The best resource a Christian communicator has is their own experience of God and what they themselves have made of that experience in their private reflections and in the way they live their life. That is what they have been given to share with other people. Yours may not seem very much compared with St Paul's conversion on the road to Damascus, or even compared with the obvious holiness of the backs of necks in the rows in front of you in Church on a Sunday morning, but it is what you have been given and for you it matters. It is your first-hand evidence and carries far more weight than your being trained to repeat correct Church teaching. So, try it out with your friend!

Formation

It is worth making a distinction between the ideas which go along with the word education and those which are to do with the word formation. For me education speaks of school and learning about subjects. Although other things are involved, (there is 'Physical Education' after all) it is largely intellectual, about retaining and using facts and concepts. It is training the mind. Instruction plays a large part in it. For most people education means being taught by a teacher.

Formation on the other hand is giving form to something, shaping it. In formation the concern is, certainly, to some extent with understanding subjects but it is far wider. Formation is about helping a person to develop into shape for which God has given them the potential. In Christian formation the first aim is not to impart doctrines about God but rather to encourage someone in their search for God, in their meeting with him and in letting their whole life be moulded and changed by that experience. Christian formation is about being transformed into the pattern of Christ.

Using formation rather than instruction as a model gives a great weight to the importance of story. As a later chapter will show, this is both letting the gospel story and the stories of our Christian tradition do their work simply as stories. That, after all, is what they are before they become transmuted into doctrines and dogmas. It also means valuing the individual personal stories of the people with whom we are travelling as important for themselves and as the scene within which God is at work in his world.

To work with story is to enter into people's experience, to invite them to reflect upon what happens to them and upon what their own actions and reactions have been in the light of the story of the Gospel. From this relating real life and God's revelation comes the challenge to change in the present and the future.

Relationship with God

The journey we are on ourselves and the journey of the people we are accompanying is a journey of faith, a journey in God and to God. The work of clergy, catechists and sponsors is not primarily to teach about the Christian religion. It is to open eyes, minds, hearts and souls to God and his love, power, goodness, truth and justice seen in the person and the work of Jesus. Our first aim is not understanding but faith. It is conversion to Christ. It is helping people to the place where, like the Ethiopian in some readings of Acts 8.37, they can say, 'I believe that Jesus Christ is Lord'. The many different aspects of the process of conversion are the subject of another part of this book. Here simply let me say that if the Church is not working for change in people's lives in response to the Gospel, it is failing in its commission from God.

Spirituality

One very important part of Christian formation is prayer and the development of spirituality. The world of the 1980s in England shows many signs of a thirst for things of the spirit. It is remarkable how many people in their search for meaning in life turn to spiritual practices like yoga or meditation, following eastern religions like Hinduism or Buddhism – or at least borrowing from their habits of spirituality. This is to say nothing of the people who look to the more modern ways of self-discovery through psychoanalysis or the deep personal conversions which lie in the heart of Alcoholics Anonymous. The occult, too, in all its manifestations, offers a sense of meaning and purpose as an answer to some people's spiritual search.

What I find sad and worrying is that, for all its centuries of devotion to things of the spirit, the Christian church (or the Christian churches, to be more accurate) are not resources to which enquirers naturally turn for help in their quest. I suspect that one reason for this among several is that Christians are not themselves confident that they have anything to give to other people. For a very large number of Church people prayer is an important part of life, but in my experience only a few feel strong enough to talk openly about it. There is a hidden conspiracy about to say that prayer is for experts to teach, rather than for 'ordinary people' to chat about. Of course there are people who are acknowledged leaders; they give retreats, write books and help individuals to grow in spirituality. But there is a real danger of a 'guru-culture' which while exalting the guru, perhaps too much, at the same time devalues the ordinary practitioner of prayer, the man and woman in the pew.

So, once again, here is an area in Christian life where the

catechumenate method encourages lay men and women to share their own experiences with other people. This accompanying others in spiritual matters also encourages the Christian to grow, to explore for himself or herself. The chapter on 'Friendship with God' is meant to whet the appetite. Clergy, members of religious communities and lay people need to be sufficiently at home in the world of prayer to help beginners. Once they discover that it is possible to dare to talk openly about an intimate relationship with God; once they experience that in a caring dialogue people can grow in their awareness of God and the ways he wants them to develop, then they may want to acquire the understanding and learn the skills that belong to spiritual direction.

Worship

Private devotion is not the Christian's only way of expressing their relationship with God. At several points in this book we return to what for many English people Christianity is mainly about – 'going to Church'. The Christian community meets for worship. Apart from the actual work of worshipping God, this also provides a shop window display of the Church. It is where the fact of Church is made manifest in the town or city or the suburb or the village. It is often where men and women come, shyly perhaps, to test whether this group of people or this priest can help them in their search for meaning.

Common worship moulds those who take part in it. It too is part of the formation of the new Christian. Therefore it needs to be both attractive and true to all that Christian discipleship means.

Christian Tradition

My emphasis on formation rather than instruction does not mean that I ignore the inheritance of belief and practice which is to be found in Church and Bible. To talk about leading people to faith in God, does not wipe out talk about 'The Faith', it simply puts it in a different place.

As people come to faith in Christ they have to face the fact of the Church. Their route to faith will almost certainly be marked by their encounters at different times of their life with members of the Church, official or lay who have either hindered them or helped them forward on their journey. For some the fact of the Church as they have met it or as they imagine it is a barrier. Jesus may attract them but they are put off by his people or by the organisation which represents him in today's world. On the other hand there are men and women who find an attraction in the life of the Church and look for friendship among the people who belong to it.

I have a vivid memory of asking a candidate for baptism and confirmation what made her take the step of asking for it. She had first approached the Church to have her baby christened and she replied, 'The lady who came round from the Church to talk about the christening had got something and I wanted it too'.

The Church is often seen quite simply as a place to find friends, somewhere to go if you are lonely. It is an institution which is thought to be in the business of offering help, of offering healing to people who are hurt.

Sacraments

If the journey towards faith in God through Jesus Christ is also a journey towards the sacraments of Christian initiation, then it is a journey towards joining the Church. Christian baptism, as well as being baptism into the one, holy, catholic and apostolic Church is also baptism into the local manifestation of that wonderful body – the Church where you and I worship, where we are members and where we are called to exercise our ministry. People who are on their journey towards baptism will need to get to know the people and the life of that Church. They will take part in its worship and in the social events and neighbourhood service which the community offers.

The Local Church

The trouble is that they will meet, not some ideal Christian community, but the strange mixture of people and the even stranger set of habits, attitudes and cross-currents of emotion which mark the congregation at the Parish Church in the High Street.

This faces the local Church fairly and squarely with the need to ask itself whether the story it has to tell and which its life displays is a true reflection of the gospel story. Can the newcomer see a line of continuity between the Jesus he or she meets in the New Testament and the Church of Jesus which meets in the Parish Church? There is a whole range of qualities which a community could well take note of. Is the Church welcoming or cold? I mean the people even more than the building! Are they open or closed? What about the unity of the Church? Is it cliquey and do people cherish factions and resentments? Where is the attention of the community focussed, on self-preservation or concern for people outside the fellowship? Is there a sense of a desire for God, his worship and his service which runs deep or is there a suspicion of superficiality? What sort of people belong? Is there a sense of selection or of preconditions for entry?

In this kind of self-examination members of the Church need to look both at what is public, the worship, the activities, the organizations and the involvement in society and also at the more private assumptions about patterns of responsibility and authority and about the different layers of needs met and help offered by the Church. I mention all this as Christian tradition because it is the tradition which the enquirer sees. The established lay person and even more the trained and educated minister may well think of the tradition of beliefs and liturgy, of culture, history and doctrine which are part of the inheritance to be shared with the newcomers of this generation. These are all important, they are part of the story we have to tell. As someone goes through the process of joining the community they need to get to know at least some part of the story and to make it their own. However what an enquirer looks for is some kind of agreement and harmony in the Christian community between the behaviour of that community and its gospel. It is against this practical testing that those who are accompanying enquirers have to share their faith, helping them to enter into the inheritance of what it means to be a Christian and a member of the Church.

There is a Christian inheritance, a living tradition of revelation which seeks in every generation to present the story of God's dealing with his creation to the people of that generation in a way which is both true to the tradition and relevant and challenging to contemporary people. The catechist or the sponsor needs to be enough at home within the tradition to be able to hear and feel the relevance of the Christian story to their own lives and to the life of the society in which they live. They need to have enough confidence and sensitive perception to relate the tradition-story with the story told them by the person they are accompanying. This is, I believe, the work of practical, local theology. It is open to clergy and lay alike.

3

Faith and Believing

'It is Jesus Christ I believe in most. He lived like us; he knew poverty and want; he experienced what is true for people, what it means to be a person. Jesus didn't bother about the noise the crowd was making – he only heard the blind man. He was strong; not weak like us. He died having fulfilled what he had to fulfil, still with his strength and his faith. I want to have this strength, which I haven't yet got.

'Jesus is not dead. For me it's not finished. I hope when I die to be with him. For me he is always there.

'It's Jesus who makes God real for us.

'I always wanted to go to Church as a girl, but my family was against it. I found the opportunity when I came to ask for my babies to be christened. I have been helped by a priest and this group of friends.

'My mother's death helped me towards faith. I'm sure I will meet her.

It was in Northern France that I sat in on an evening session with the small group of people accompanying a young mother of two children. She worked as a bank clerk. Her baptism was in a few weeks and together they were preparing her 'Profession of Faith'. At Epiphany as she stood before the water she would be asked to affirm her belief in her own words, along the lines of those notes which I took at the time.

Faith is what being a Christian is about, but like so many

vitally important things in life people are uncertain about exactly what it means. They build up all sorts of different personal and shared images about it. We are concerned with the work of accompanying people to that place on their journey where they can make their own commitment to the faith of the community they desire to join.

The work of adult catechesis is to be found in the process of welcome, conversion and nurture. It depends both on the method and the material content used in that process. I put method first because it is essential to recognise that the approach is concerned with people; programme or syllabus come second. We are not dealing with a course of instruction; it is journeys, each individual person making their own. The method has to model this.

The task of the Christian guide and friend is to foster and provide for dialogue, meeting, creative confrontation between the person, who comes with his or her own story of life, events and relationships, and the Church's story of God's revelation of himself in the created world, in the life, death and resurrection of Jesus Christ and the continuing life of his people. Later in this chapter I shall suggest some methods by which this can be achieved. For the moment I simply point out that there is an infinite variety of ways of helping people meet God and be changed by him. They involve every side of human personality. Sometimes it is through one-to-one conversation; sometimes it is through meeting God's people as a community. It could be the experience of worship or the healing brought by forgiveness and acceptance. The dialogue is between individuals with their own story, their gifts and their requests and the Gospel as told by and lived in the Church. There is a place for wonder and awe, for the excitement of new discoveries of meaning and relationship, for falling in love with Jesus, for letting God's love, truth and justice challenge and reshape the attitudes and responses of everyday life.

More than teaching people about the Christian faith so that

they understand it, what we are about is a process of learning, growing and changing which involves the whole person and which affects every aspect of their life, private and public. Of course in this life it never can achieve its fulfilment. Here in the preparation of people for baptism and confirmation we are dealing with the opening stages. However we are right to expect it to make a difference in people. Indeed one of the areas of enquiry to see if people are ready for initiation is around the question whether their life and behaviour shows signs of Christian commitment. I have a vivid memory of a man with his own small engineering company who said to me, 'Peter, I don't know if I ought to be confirmed. I'm not sure what difference it will make to the way I run my business.'

Faith

There is a family connection between the words and phrases we use: 'A meaning to life', 'A purpose in life', 'A faith' or 'The Faith'. They all have to do with our making sense of ourselves and people and things around us: or, indeed, being unable to come to terms. They are about 'The way you lean into life'. It is presenting to ourselves what really matters to us. Turn all or any of these into areas of human search, questioning, pain or fear and you find the roots of most of the requests for help which people bring to the Church, its members or its ministers.

The Christian response is to invite the enquirer in one way or another to share in the Christian faith. I say 'in one way or another' because there is a wide variety of personalities and a wide range of life-stories. Both will influence someone in their perception of what matters for them in the cluster of meanings around the nucleus of the Christian faith. This is one of those occasions when I wish the following pages could be accompanied by a videotape of animated graphics. Faith is dynamic and relational rather than analytical and static. So please bear that in mind as you read on.

'Belief that . . .'

When Philip the deacon baptized the Ethiopian eunuch the condition 'If you believe that Jesus Christ is Lord' looks like the earliest form of test for Christian initiation. From it developed the Creeds as we have them, the Apostles' Creed growing from the baptismal creed of the Church in Rome and the Nicene Creed developing through the processes of Ecumenical Councils of Bishops in the Church to define the Orthodox Catholic Faith in the face of different heresies.

For some people the Christian faith consists of their ability to recite the Creed and mean it wholeheartedly. Among a certain range of members of the Church of England there is a feeling of standing to attention during the saying of the Creed in Church, not far removed from the feeling of the National Anthem or the Last Post on Remembrance Sunday at the two minutes' silence. The words matter. They express the truth and demand assent. Here are a series of beliefs about God and Jesus expressed in summary form as the essentials of the faith.

'Relationship with . . .'

Not so much 'believing that . . .' as 'trusting in . . .' is another approach to faith with a different emphasis. Jesus endorsed the two short summaries of the Jewish Law, 'Love God with all your heart and mind and strength', and 'Love your neighbour as yourself'. Christian faith is seen not so much in the intellectual assent to doctrine as in the commitment of the will to respond to the love of God by loving him in return, following the example of the Jesus seen in the Gospels and entering into a relationship with the Father through him and in his spirit.

This relationship with God overflows and finds its practical expression in a life lived in obedience to the teachings of Jesus. Christian faith implies Christian living. The Gospels are full of the insistence of Jesus that, unlike the Pharisees, his disciples were to live out their belief in God's love by sharing love with others. There is an essential practicality about being a Christian. Belief in the incarnation, that God took human flesh, demands that it is in the choices and relationships of human life and human society that faith is to be realised.

Belonging

Christian faith is the faith of the Christian community. The gospels record the story told by that community; the Creeds are its summaries and its existence bears witness to a desire to live obedient to the command to love one's neighbour.

Whether it is seen from a 'high' belief in the Church as the Body of Christ or a 'low' belief in the Church as a community of believers, Christian history shows that the faith is essentially a community experience. Jesus did not leave behind a set of rules or a code of doctrine; he left a group of people. What gives this group and its successors meaning and cohesion is the story we tell. The story of the Good News is in our books, summarised in our Creeds and is the ideal by which we try to live our own lives as a community and as individuals.

Many Christians naturally define themselves as Christians not by the beliefs they hold but by their church allegiance, either to a denomination or to a particular local congregation 'I'm a Methodist' or 'I go to St. John's'. Belonging matters. Faith is a corporate event in their lives and is as intimately connected with friendships and group loyalties as with belief or behaviour.

Balanced Faith

Clearly none of these aspects, intellectual assent, relationship with God and its overflowing into lifestyle and community, are mutually exclusive. It is not a question of either/or. Far from it; a balanced Christian faith contains them all and each gives shape to or expresses the others. At different stages of development and in different types of person one or other

aspect of faith will predominate. When one aspect grows out
of all proportion and swamps the others, there is a distortion.

Among Anglicans there has, I suspect, long been a heavy
reliance on assent to the written statements of belief and a
comparative neglect of the other two. An emphasis on books
and reading; churchgoers who feel lost if they cannot follow
the Service for themselves from the page in front of them; and
a certain mystique of the priest as one who has studied
theology – all these tend to result in a down-grading of faith
as relationship and belonging.

I am concerned to restore the lost balance and to give full
weight to the non-verbal, non-intellectual side of Christian
faith experience. The process followed in formation of adult
Christians matters as much as the content. People learn by
example and by experience as much as (or more than) by
persuasion or explanation. The method used in adult catechesis should reflect and incarnate the belief that God cares for
and gives infinite value to each man and woman.

Norbert Mette writing on *The Christian Community's Task
in the Process of Religious Education* describes six aspects:
'(a) Learning the faith is a total process of learning that
involves the whole man or woman. The invitation to disci-
pleship and the challenge to conversion cannot be compart-
mentalized, but affects all spheres of life. The aim of learning
the faith is becoming a responsible agent, is man's or woman's
"integral liberation". This rules out every form of compulsion
and manipulation.
'(b) Learning the faith is a process that lasts as long as life
itself. It follows the course of human development and encourages it by continually challenging one to become personally aware of and appropriate the fullness of life with the
promise it offers.
'(c) Learning the faith is a process that transcends the genera-
tions and a mutual process in which those involved learn from
each other . . .
'(d) Learning the faith is a process of learning in solidarity. It
takes place when faith and life are shared among each other
and interpreted jointly in the light of the biblical message.

.

'(e) Learning the faith is a committed process of learning. Learning to grasp the possibilities of life given by God makes one sensitive to everyone deprived of the elementary rights of living and bringing one's life to fulfilment.

'(f) Learning the faith is an innovatory process of learning. It does not simply limit itself to instruction in current values and norms. Rather it arouses at the same time the ability to examine them to see whether they make human life possible and in certain cases to change them.'[1]

Process and Content

In ordinary everyday relationships and conversation the actual words we say to one another form only a part of the interchange between people. The content, the message carried by words is reinforced or denied by many other facets of communication. Gesture, facial expression, tone of voice, social accent, even clothes, each carry their own strong message. We may hear and understand what someone says, but what we remember is the kind of person they showed themselves to be and the overall impression they made on us. We look for answers to questions such as, 'Do I trust her?'; 'Does he like me?'; 'Am I safe here?'; 'Is he listening to what I have to say?'.

Communicating Christian faith is no different. Certainly there are people who have met Christ and been changed as people through the printed word alone, but I suspect they are few and far between. The normal way to learn and grow, the way to conversion is by way of meeting with other people and being open to their influence.

This is why I believe that the way adult formation takes place is as important as the content of the teaching which is given. Throughout this book I have in mind the model of working with a group of people, probably no more than eight or ten. It is small enough for a certain intimacy and large enough to give some variety of experience and attitudes. I suggest there will be either one or two leaders who have some ability to work in and with a group and who are mature enough in their own faith and knowledge to help others with some confidence (though not, I hope, with overweening self-assurance!). Some members of the group are Christian helpers, already partway along the journey and the rest are those for whom the group has come into being, the enquirers and people on their way towards Christian commitment, faith and initiation. The kind of life experienced in this group has as much effect as the content of the syllabus. As simple evidence for this I merely ask you to look back over your own life, reflect upon times of learning in church and ask what stands out in your memory, what has had the most influence. I should be surprised if it is not more the people and their attitude or events and feelings about them rather than items of knowledge or insight into doctrines which come strongly to mind.

In the church as anywhere else there is always a danger that good ideas get over-used or misused and strong words end up as jargon buzz-words. I worry about the words 'share' and 'story'. They could be facing this danger, but I want to use them and to enter quite deeply into their meanings and connections.

I envisage the enquirer learning about God and finding faith in him through his or her encounter and developing a relationship with the people of Jesus. For this to happen there must be a situation where they can actually be welcomed, be met as individuals and be accepted. It is most unlikely that this can be found in church services or in large gatherings. It does happen in individual encounters; one-to-one conversations and friendships are very much part of most people's maturing as Christians. They involve to a greater or lesser extent each person in openness about themselves and accepting the other for what they are. 'Sharing' is the shorthand for what happens when people talk in that way. It involves being willing to speak about one's life, one's experiences, feelings, insights and expectations within an assurance of a proper confidentiality and a trust in the other's sincerity.

The same conditions apply to the sharing within a group.

Trust is essential and it has to be earned or merited. People must not be forced into confidences they are not ready to share or burdened with other people's problems they are not willing to carry. On the other hand it is part of the natural bonding between individuals that they are willing to expose their lives, their personalities – even their names to one another.

In a Christian group journeying towards faith and commitment this bonding counts for more than a simple exercise in inter-personal dynamics. It is an experience of and a witness to God's love in accepting and forgiving men and women. It involves leaders and members in all the human skills of tact, delicacy and friendship. It also calls for the exercise of prayer and a continual desire to be open to the leading of the Holy Spirit in the work of his Church.

'Story' is shorthand for talk about someone's life with its events and relationships. It means listening to what they see as their high and low points; what matters most to them; what their interests and concerns are. Story in this sense is what gives to each person their meaning and identity. Part of it is narrative – the story told – and part is in the weight of feeling and personal investment given to different incidents or relationships or hopes and fears. It stands for this woman or this man as the person they are with all they have and bring with them into an encounter with someone else. It could be a long life-history. It could be an intense single experience which at the time is all important.

Part of the work of the group is to give value to each member's story. Apart from the natural building of friendship and trust, this valuing is essential in a Christian group for two reasons. It is again, evidence that each individual has infinite value to God and so to his Church. 'I need to know by experiencing it that I matter.' It is also a vital part in the work of Christian formation to recognise God at work in the ordinary, everyday life of each person. God can be seen at work in very ordinary situations and events.

There are two streets in North London, parallel turnings off a suburban High Street. The houses were very much the same, built as part of a 1920s development, but one was a friendly, neighbourhood street and the other was cold. When I asked why the difference, the people in the friendly street told me about a woman who'd lived there some years before. Whenever a new person or family moved in she went round with a bunch of flowers. Although she had died, the neighbours kept up the habit.

Gerry told me his story. His wife had left him for a man at the firm she worked for. He had taken it hard, got very depressed and drank too much. He'd thought of suicide. His boss was complaining about him. What changed all this was a friend who just asked him if he would like to go fishing the next weekend. He felt someone had noticed – and he enjoyed sitting peacefully by the canal beginning to sort himself out.

The Jewish-Christian vision is of a God who is Creator and Judge responsible for and active in the life of people and communities in his world; a God who in Jesus Christ has entered fully into all that it means to be human to redeem humanity. So it is right to give high importance to individual lives as the place where vocation is at work, the process of God's call and human response in and through the events of childhood and youth, work and leisure, marriage or singleness, maturity and old age, birth and bereavement.

The third of the elements in the process of Christian formation as I see it, along with the life and dynamics of the group itself and the sharing of the stories of the members, is the Gospel, the Bible story or the Church's story. It is what we as followers of Jesus have to tell about him and what he shows us of God. Here is where we enter the realm of the books of instruction about the Christian faith, the beginners' guides to the teachings of the Church. But, once again, I want to plead for narrative rather than analysis.

John Westerhoff writes: 'Our identity is dependent on having a story that tells us who we are. Our understanding of life's meaning and purpose is dependent on having a story that tells us what the world is like and where we are going. To be a community of faith we must be a people with a story, a common memory and vision, common rituals and symbols expressive of our community's memory and vision and a common life together that manifests our community's memory and vision. The Church is a story-formed community.'[2]

To put it over-simply: What gives the Jewish faith of the Old Testament its strength is the covenant story (or stories) with the continuing account of God's involvement in the history of his people. It reaches its peak in the saving event of the Exodus, combined with the demand that his people respond by life lived in accordance with his Law.

What the New Testament calls for is a faith-response to the story of Jesus, seen as God's Messiah, crucified and raised from death. His story includes, of course, stories of his Ministry, teaching, parables, signs and miracles as well as the continuing story of his followers in the letters and the Acts of the Apostles. It is retold and re-experienced in each successive generation of the Christian Church.

One particular way the Church tells its story is in the keeping of the Christian year. The church calendar acts out the Gospel and the Sunday readings in the different cycles in use in the churches provide a resource of material to base the work of a group on.

Story-Gospel Dialogue

'Our first task in approaching another people, another culture, another religion is to take off our shoes, for the place we are approaching is holy; else we might find ourselves treading on another's dream. More serious still, we may forget that God was there before us.' I saw these words in a wall poster at a centre preparing volunteer missionaries for service in the Third World. They are as true for the ministry of the Christian accompanying someone into faith along the lines we are dealing with here. The dialogue between the Church and the enquirer, between the Gospel and the person's story begins with the Church listening to the enquirer. The leader helps the newcomer to tell their story and tries to listen and discern with love and attention both to the man or woman speaking and to God who is and has been active in their history.

Listening

It is not difficult to listen to someone else's story. To do it well may take a bit of practice, because it is not something everyone is good at. Most people seem to find it easier to talk than to listen! In fact once you set yourself to listen and help the other person tell their story simply by giving your attention, you will find it intensely interesting. This is usually a surprise to the story-teller because he or she thinks their own life dull and ordinary!

It will be clear by now that what I mean by 'Story' is rather wider than a simple recounting of events. It covers what is important to the person; what he would like me to know about himself; what she has weighing on her mind this evening.

If you invite someone, 'Tell me a little about yourself', expect all sorts of answers. 'I was born in Pontyprydd and my parents moved up to Streatham when I was three because my father lost his job in South Wales and came up to London to find work.' 'My husband and I have got three children at school so I don't go out to work any more.' 'I am a stewardess on short-haul flights. It's all right but you get very tired in the summer'. 'I don't know, life seems rather a mess at the moment. Since we split up, nothing's going right. I get very anxious and depressed.' 'I've got a job at Robinson's, in the paint shop. There's my two brothers in the firm. It's where the family's always worked.'

Just five possible answers are an indication. As you read you can think of scores of others. How do you answer a question like that yourself? What do your close friends say? Can you think of recent conversations with people you have met? As you reflect on the answers I suggest you may begin to ask what they show about the speaker's sense of and meaning in life. What matters to them? What are their deeper questions? The description people give to their own story or the tone in which they tell it may well point to how they judge the meaning and purpose in their life at that moment. The value they give to their own past, their childhood, parents and grandparents. The value they put on themselves – 'I'm afraid I'm only a housewife'.

Status in life is important for most people. It is about the image we have of ourselves. Many factors go to a sense of status. From within there is a personal sense of worth, of being someone; or of lostness, being unwanted. Externally there are different sorts of achievement, at work, in family life, among friends. There are the indicators which mark social status; size of house and the class of neighbourhood speak volumes to other people.

The work of a good leader of a group or a friend accompanying an enquirer towards faith begins with these stories. There is common ground there. Maybe the events and the personalities are not common to everyone – it would be surprising if they were. But what is common is the living of life and the being affected by the relationships and events of life. It is vital to be able to listen well. The leader needs to encourage and reassure and reinforce without telling too much of their own story. A danger is in the natural desire to swop excitements and to cap the other person's tale with one of our own. Resist this urge! It may sometimes be suitable, but only rarely. What is called for is the ability to give attention and to draw out what really matters for each person in the group. Beyond that and deeper into the heart of the process is a need for discernment, first in order to see the high points and the depths in someone's telling of their story, and then to be able to suggest where in the story God is to be encountered, who is the meaning of life.

Stories of Faith

As people tell their story they may well talk about their beliefs and their awareness of God for themselves. Many will have a 'pre-history' of contact with the Church, perhaps as a child in

Sunday School or through a family funeral or a wedding. They will have faced situations in their lives when they have asked deep questions or have been moved by experiences they cannot quite explain.

Leaders need not only to encourage, listen and discuss. They also need to respond appropriately with the Christian story. At times and probably more often as the journey moves forward towards deeper commitment and awareness on the part of the enquirers, the group sessions will begin from Gospel and move towards life story, rather than the other way. Whichever direction the dialogue takes it does call for a degree of knowledge of the Christian tradition and a certain agility on the part of the leader to move about the material and select what is suitable.

Joan is a single woman. She lives at home and cares for her mother who is an invalid. She goes out to work at an office job which is safe but dull. She dislikes it, but can't face the thought of moving to a new firm. Anyway she might not find one. She feels stuck and flat – and not a little angry. Her life seems less than it could be.

The group leader asks what the Gospel has to say to Joan in this particular time. Who did Jesus meet who felt like Joan? What story seems appropriate? As you read, you might like for a moment to put the book down and ask yourself those questions.

You may well come up with something quite different from me. I simply suggest that there is something in Joan's story about being blocked, paralysed. I think it would be suitable to read or tell the story of the four friends who brought the paralysed man to Jesus and let him down into the house through the roof. The conversation could go on to the echoes and meanings which the story of the healing brings to Joan; where she can hear a connection between forgiveness and release from paralysis; what is the part played by these friends in the group; and what response she finds proper to make to the word she hears.

The range of stories and concerns is infinite from intimate

personal worries and pleasures to the military use of space. I hesitate to give too many examples. I would much rather that people who either are already working with adults or are preparing to accompany others on a faith journey used this as an opportunity to reflect on what they have heard from other people and also what they know about themselves. Let the reflection enter into underlying causes and trends and see what needs for healing, forgiveness, salvation come to the surface. Ask yourself what in your understanding of the Gospel story speaks to those needs. As well, spend some time reflecting on the story of your own journey in faith. What parts of the Gospel, the story told by the Church or lived in the Church, have been bright and alive for you, a source of saving or healing or insight.

In this I am asking people to use their skills and abilities of perception. Words like 'see', 'hear', 'realize' are more important at this point than 'think', 'analyse', 'give reasons'. That throws us back to the purpose of the exercise. What I am not talking about is a Bible Study Group, working through, say, the Gospel according to Luke with a commentary. Still less am I talking about a session on the Bible as part of a 'Bishop's Certificate' course. These, of course, have their proper place and I would hope that they formed part of the preparation of group leaders. No, here we are seeking to provide an opportunity for a meeting between God and a person, for an opening or a deepening of the person's awareness of what the Good News is for them. For this to happen we need to let the telling and listening to stories do their own work.

A friend of mine was working with a group of Cambodian refugees now settled in the U.S.A. She told the story of the people of Israel in bondage in Egypt and their escape in the Exodus. As she spoke and as one of them translated into Cambodian, their faces lit up and they became more and more excited. 'But that's our story', they said, 'We have been oppressed and persecuted. We have seen people we love killed or tortured. Now we have escaped across the water into a new country.'

We try to let the story speak and then to discuss and develop what people hear in the story. God speaks through his word and people can be helped to listen.

The Gospel is the story which gives the Church its meaning. So there is a parallel reason for story telling. It is that people who want to join the Church need to be part of that story and the identity it brings. They need to be able to sing the community songs and recognize the names of the community heroes.

As I said above, the Church year with its seasons and its festivals tells of the suffering, death and resurrection of Jesus at Easter. It tells of the empowering of his disciples to become the Church with a world-wide commission to proclaim the Gospel and baptise at Pentecost. It looks back to the Jewish Church's story of Creation and Fall, of Abraham and Moses and David, of covenant between God and man, of God who communicates in judgement and hope, punishment and forgiveness with his people. It looks forward from the story of Jesus the man, his birth and his Ministry, to the story of the Body of Christ. It commemorates the heroes of the Church of the New Testament and of the Christian centuries since. It proclaims the Christian hope for the Kingdom of God now and in the infinite future.

This is the story which the Church has to tell and to which the enquirer is invited to respond. This is the story which the enquirer rightly challenges to give meaning to his or her own life. In the telling and the hearing of this story a man or woman has every right to ask, 'Does the God who acts like this, does this Jesus who says, performs and suffers these things, speak to me in my own life? Where do my story and this story meet?'

Probably it is not going to be for most people the broad sweep of the story in the Christian year which provides the revelation and excites the wonder. Rather than the *Story* it will be the *stories* which connect. The Old and the New Testament are filled with good stories with human interest, whether it is of the journey in faith which Abraham took to an unknown country or David's shameful adultery with Bathsheba and his murder of her husband; or the call of Isaiah; or Jeremiah's proclamation of God's judgement on his own nation and his persecution because of it. In the Gospels there are the parables which Jesus told, there are the stories of his miracles, his encounters with people and the stories of his birth and of his passion, death and resurrection. They are often good stories, simply in themselves, but their purpose and their use is to engage the hearers and to draw them into relationship with God as the central character. There is a danger in working from the individual person's story that the conversation can become over-subjective. The Bible points to the wider reference, it roots human events within God's plan for his world, it sets up an external set of values to judge our reactions by.

Pictures and metaphors are a kind of miniature story. The words and images the Church uses for God are part of its story – or at any rate the language of its story. They are well worth entering into. God as Creator, Father, Redeemer. God as love, light, wind and fire. God as rock, depth, warrior. Read the hymns and hear what echoes resound in your imagination at the language without the music. Listen to Isaiah, Hosea and St. Paul. Listen to the evangelical revival preachers. Listen to the words of the liturgy and let the names of God work on your deep needs or highest aspirations and those of the people you are accompanying. Which names sing for you and which are empty?

Starting from the Gospel

There is no one right way to help people to hear God speaking to their lives through the Bible. In this Section what I offer is simply ideas on which each leader will base their own group sessions, always leaving room for adaptation in response both to what they hear themselves in their reading and to what the members of their group ask for.

Preparation is vital. I am indebted to Karen Hinman Powell

of the North American Forum on the Catechumenate for her
stages of preparation, designed for a Sunday morning catechetical session following the Ministry of the Word and here
slightly edited for more general use. The leader is encouraged
to follow these steps. No one can guide anyone else unless
they have been there themselves before! If leaders are working
in pairs, then this preparation should ideally be done together,
allowing plenty of time for individual silent reflection as well
as time for sharing insights and practical planning:

1. Find the readings. If you are following the pattern of the
Sunday Cycle, this means reading through all three readings
slowly and thoughtfully at least three times. Underline words
or phrases that strike you as significant. Make a note of
connections between the different readings. Get to know what
is there in them.

2. Now enter into the Gospel. Read it over slowly and
deliberately again. Picture it in your mind or imagination.
Where does it take place? What time of day? What season of
the year? Does place or time make a difference to the story?
Who are the characters in the story? What are their names?
Who do you find you identify with?

Who is the principal person in the Gospel story? What is
their problem or their interest? Find in the text a phrase which
expresses this from their perspective. (It is imperative to
discover all this from *within* the Gospel.)

What is Jesus' response? How does he meet the interest or
deal with the problem? (Again, find the answer in the text.)
How do the other characters respond to the situation.

In all this try to place yourself in the text, experience it
through the senses of your imagination – touch, sight, smell,
hearing.

3. Once you have finished this visualizing and entering into
the text and not before, read commentaries on the passage
and let your mind work on it. How do the commentator's
notes enlarge your understanding or challenge your perception of the Gospel?

4. Then leave all the reading, visualizing and thinking with

commentaries on one side and come before God to pray in and with this Gospel. You may find yourself listening for answers to questions like, What do these readings mean to you in your life? What do you hear Jesus saying to you (perhaps in your identification with one of the characters)? Are there strong echoes in your memory of incidents or people in your own life and experience? If there are, recall them carefully before God in the light of the Gospel. What are the connections? How do you respond? What does all this tell you about God, about Jesus, about yourself?

5. With all you have so far gathered, ask what questions are raised about the Christian tradition, the teachings of the Church and the life of the Christian community to which you belong.

6. Then design the outline of your group session and get together any materials that will be needed. Think which texts you are going to use. Work out a basic timetable. Design the layout of the room you will be in with any pictures or objects you want as a focus for prayer or reflection.

Three Models

These three patterns which follow are a resource to draw from. They have been designed with an awareness of the way adults learn and mature; they are specifically aimed at relating life and Gospel and they have been tested over a long time of experience.

An African Model

1 Opening prayer to gather the members together and focus the session.
2 Read the Gospel aloud slowly and deliberately. Ask people to listen for a word or phrase that stands out or speaks for them.
3 One minute of silence.

4 Invite everyone simply to say the word or phrase that touched them. Do not discuss!

5 Read the Gospel again.

6 Tell the group you will give them five minutes of silence to be with the Gospel (or three minutes if they are new to it). Be quiet for that time.

7 Invite them to note down what they hear in their heart, what the passage says that touches their life.

8 Divide into groups of not more than four or five, perhaps twos or threes, to speak of what they have got from the Gospel. It is very important that they use the word 'I' and own their personal experience and insight, rather than say what others believe. It is not a time for discussing or preaching or solving the problems of other people.

9 Read the Gospel again.

10 Ask people to consider what, in the light of the meeting so far, they believe God wants from them this week. How is he inviting them to change? What are they taking home with them this week? Specific answers are important, rather than responses like 'God wants me to be good for ever and ever'!

11 Again in little groups share these answers.

12 Gather the group together for a closing prayer with perhaps one of the readings, open prayer, silence or singing.

13 Give details of the next meeting and the passages to be read.

St Augustine's Church, Washington DC

Raymond Kemp suggests the following pattern.

1 Opening prayer, to include a reading of the Gospel.

2 Invite people to write their responses to the following questions:

(i) What did you hear? Write three thoughts, ideas, phrases, images that grabbed you in the reading.

(ii) What does it mean? Why did these words or images grab you today? What do they mean for your life? Can you recall a time in your life (past or present) which you experienced something similar to the event in today's reading? How does the reading enlighten or challenge that experience?

Write three questions that today's reading raises for you about your life, about your faith, about Church . . .

(iii) What does it cost you to live this message?

Note one concrete way you feel called to live this message this week.

What will help you to live this? What will be the obstacles?

3 Divide into small groups for members to share their reflections with each other.

4 All together in one group share insights learned and any questions left unresolved.

5 Closing Prayer.

6 Arrangements for next meeting.

Karen Hinman Powell's Model

1 Opening Prayer to include reading of the Gospel.

2 Reflections on the Gospel. Ask people to make notes:

(i) List three or four ideas, images or thoughts that struck them in today's reading.

(ii) Describe a time in the past week when they were called to live out one of these ideas. How did they respond?

(iii) Write down two questions the reading raises for them about being a Christian.

3 Share these reflections in small groups of four to six people.

4 In the large group feed back the experiences in small groups. In particular ask what similarities and differences they found; what questions do they have as a

group about the Christian tradition and the Church (list these questions on a board).

5 (Optional) A short input by the leader on one or more of these issues, either a spontaneous response or prepared beforehand.

6 Discussion on the input.

7 Quiet reflection. Ask people to name one concrete way in which they feel challenged to live differently this week. Let the changes start small, definite and limited.

8 Share this with one or two people.

9 Closing prayer.

10 Arrangements for next time.[3]

The Context

In some places the catechumenal session takes place on Sunday at the time of the main eucharist. Following the ancient pattern the people who are preparing for initiation take part in the Ministry of the Word, the reading and the sermon and then withdraw for their 'Breaking of the Word' while the rest of the Church goes on to the Breaking of the Bread. Where this happens, there is further material for people to work on from the sermon in the Service and preacher and the leaders of the session on the Gospel may well want to prepare, if not actually together, at least with some reference to one another.

Group Life

It is not my intention in this section to train people to lead groups. That simply is not possible in a book. The skills and attitudes needed in a good group leader have to be acquired or developed in practice and with personal guidance, teaching and review. As with so much else in what I am putting forward, it is as much a matter of experience and talking over actual events and relationships as of learning the principles and techniques beforehand.

Along with most of the things in life, working in small

groups has its pluses and its minuses so it is worth noting some of them and underlining a few of the points already made.

The Positive

A group of up to, say, a dozen people provides what a congregation often cannot, a human-sized community. It is small enough for members to get to know each other well, large enough to provide both a variety of characters and temperaments and also space for individuals to relax and rest. It is where people can find human relationships within the Church. Rather than be taught about Christian love, they can actually experience it. Anne, after a year or so in a group leading on to confirmation, said, 'I very much valued being taken seriously, being properly listened to, not being ridiculed'. There is a sense of safety, of the support which is given and received by people who have begun to care for and about one another.

In the group as an experience of what it means to be Church there is fellowship which includes two essential elements in the Christian life. One is forgiveness. Sometimes it may be a very clear expression of repentance for a wrong done and the assurance of God's love and the love of the members of the group. Sometimes it is the less formal but no less real experience of being accepted for oneself with one's faults and difficulties, of being given value as someone loved by God.

With all this a small group can be the place to foster growth into Christian maturity. Debbie wrote, 'In our group over eighteen months, I believe we have all grown in patience with each other, especially the men for the women. We are more inclined to listen to each other and try to make helpful suggestions about personal problems. This is where comparison with the Gospel has been drawn. One of the men said he'd grown in confidence since coming to the group. He has, and it shows.' People are able to be open to others and to them-

selves. They can be seen to develop towards achieving their
own potential. 'I know how much I have grown since becoming confirmed. It is lovely to watch others who go through
these groups becoming more mature as Christian people
within the Church and in the community.'

The Negative

There are dangers too, both within the working of the group
itself and in its relationship with the wider Christian community. Small groups are open to several forms of manipulation. A leader can exercise power over members for good or
ill. It is possible to restrict and distort and so to reduce the
freedom of people to grow in their own way. The imposition
of standards and expectations, proper though this is in an
institution which does have standards and expectations, needs
very careful watching to make sure it does not tend towards
some kind of tyranny. Individual members can manipulate
too. There may be people with crying needs for recognition or
obsessive hobby-horses who can disrupt the relationships and
the work of the group as they hog the time and the attention
of the people they are with.

A person's privacy needs to be respected. There are people
for whom it is not natural to expose their all among comparative strangers. There are those who are hurt or vulnerable;
they have the right to be silent or to withdraw. Others may
rightly or wrongly not trust the confidentiality of the people in
the group and be unwilling to talk about intimate matters for
fear of gossip.

Group pressure is a force to be reckoned with among adults
almost as much as among children and adolescents. There is
an urge among many to conform. I remember one group of
men who realized the danger of this when it came to decisions
about whether or not two members should in fact go forward
to confirmation with the others. They both had reservations
and everyone in the group gave assurances that nobody was
to feel pressured or a failure if they decided against and that

they would all support each other's choices. In the event the two did decide to wait and were confirmed nine months later. But it showed how much care needs to be taken.

Although I spoke of the group as the place for growth into maturity, it is also possible for it to be the place where people can be kept in immature dependence, whether as followers of a strong leader or as companions in a tightly dependent group that dare not finish or divide up.

As far as the wider life of the congregation is concerned, I doubt whether any Church person, let alone any Vicar, is unaware of the danger of cliques. It is not uncommon for a particular group to be regarded as arrogant and exclusive by other people. Nor is it unknown for members of that group to feel that they are in fact the real Christians because of the specialness of their fellowship. Obviously this needs watching in any church. All I can offer is that over twelve years working in this way in a parish there was little sign of it, I think for two reasons. The first was that the Church was not in the habit of tolerating cliques in any case. But secondly there was no doubt that the groups had their special purpose in welcoming and preparing adult confirmation candidates and this aim was generally recognized and accepted. They were not a threat.

The groups of the sort we are describing need leaders. I suggest that it is better to have a couple of people as leaders, but that is just my suggestion. In any case leaders have a responsibility to help the group and its members to function well.

The diagram of three interlocking circles has stood the test of time. Any group leader needs to be aware of the three things to which he or she has to give attention. The group has a task to achieve. In our case it is the accompaniment of people to Christian faith and initiation. Each individual in the group is important and the leader is concerned for them, to ensure their comfort, their opportunities to put their point of view, whether they are people who need encouragement or restraint. The maintenance of the group is the third concern.

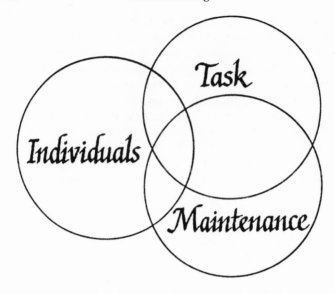

The leader needs to be aware of the relationships and the pressures within the group as well as the practical factors which will help or impede. It matters how chairs are set, whether coffee is served before, during or after the main work of a session and what time of day or day of the week suits most people.

The Bible – True or False

I have been outlining a responsible ministry for people who are to lead others along a journey of faith and into a dialogue with the Word of God met in the Gospel. They will recognize their own need to grow in faith and to develop their understanding of the Christian tradition. Bishop's Certificate Courses, lay training, Christian Institutes and similar agencies and events are available to meet this need in many places around the country.

What many people who undertake study of their Christian origins will discover is that the Bible is not as simple a source as they once thought. Someone said to me, 'I'm worried about what all this learning about the Gospels and their make-up is doing to my Jesus'. Once people enter into the world of Biblical criticism they begin to discover that it is possible to ask questions about whether the events in the Gospel happened as they are described or not, finding discrepancies between different Gospels, and the whole range of new ideas which face a student of the Bible. There is a real dilemma for many in how to present stories from the Bible for new enquirers.

Literalism has its followers in every generation. It amazes me that there should in the twentieth century be any problem over the Genesis creation stories, but I find that I have regularly to work through the different ways of expressing what is true about the world we live in. That it is the result (probably) of a big bang; that it belongs to a small solar system which is a little part of an expanding universe; that it is God's world; that it is unfair and in a mess; and that God loves us. Even so Adam and Eve are easier to deal with than questions about the Virgin Birth or Jesus walking on water.

What always needs to be remembered is that the intention of the writers, compilers, editors and users of the stories in the Bible was and is to convey truth. The means they use may be factual reporting, poetry, myth or just a good tale. God can meet us in our story through all of these. Certainly for some people it matters intensely that their search should be an intellectually responsible journey. They will rightly want to test evidence. For others story will speak to story in a way which engages quite different faculties.

In the Church of today we have rather lost faith in the power of Bible stories to do their work as stories. We are so given to analysing, explaining and cross-referring. There is ancient precedent for this, as you can see in the way in which Jesus' parable of the sower, a good story in itself, is explained a few verses later.

No, what I am suggesting is that you tell one of the parables, say the Labourers in the Vineyard or the Prodigal

Son, and simply let people respond with what the story says to
them and where it leads them on to. There may well be a good
deal of resentment about being unfairly treated or expressions
of jealousy. Rejection bites deep into people, as does being
forgiven. There are widely differing feelings about fathers and
fatherhood, just as there are about employers and workers
and the job market. Any of these and many other ideas may
come in answer to those two stories and provide more than
enough for a group to work on.

Often silence is more valuable than talk. People need space
to do the hard and deep personal work of reflecting and
accepting challenge of the Gospel story. The wise friend will
always make further space for people who need to share their
discoveries to offer their insights or to express their fear, pain
or joy. It is not my intention to teach leaders how to run
groups. The skills of a group leader cannot be learned from a
book. No more can the kind of sensitivity and awareness
which I am suggesting are needed in this work of accompanying another on a journey into faith. At the risk of being
repetitive I urge that people who are invited to take up this
ministry use every opportunity to experience this kind of
story-dialogue for themselves. Let it be something which finds
its place in a prayer group or in conversation between friends
where reflection and open sharing are possible. Again, listen
not only to the front part of your mind, the part which asks
questions and gives answers and explanations; listen to the
feelings and echoes and memories; let them have their proper
important place.

Church Habits

Experts use words like 'socialization' or 'enculturation' to
describe one aspect of education. It means being trained,
encouraged or led to adopt and be at home in the manners,
attitudes and habits of a society or a group. It is part of
anyone's life in virtually any context, whether it is to do with
what clothes to wear on this particular golf course; how not

to feel out of place when you go to tea with the girl friend's parents; keeping to your position in the bus queue; or not using that kind of language in this office! The content of adult growth into Christian faith and commitment will naturally include a certain amount of learning about the community ways of the Church and learning to conform to its expectations. This can be about the little things of Church worship, the candles, the names for people and things, sitting or kneeling and how to find your place in the right service book. It may be much deeper about community attitudes, about Church as representing a certain class or about whether gay couples are welcome in church or the relationship between our Church and the R.Cs. on the opposite corner.

Learning how to fit into the way a Christian community behaves is quite a subtle business. Sometimes you can ask straight questions if you feel lost and get clear answers from people. Sometimes it is more difficult because the habits of a community build up over a long time, often without their causes being obvious. This needs to be recognized, as I said earlier, because people who are looking to the Church for help in finding a purpose and meaning in their lives have a right to expect that the life of the Church should reflect the Gospel it professes.

It is not all one-way, of course. New people joining a community bring their own gifts and insights. Their presence and their questions may well challenge or change some of those habits and attitudes.

4

Friendship with God

'Spiritual Direction' is what happens when one Christian is helping another to grow in their discipleship. I want to use the title in the widest possible way. Used narrowly it can mean a formalized relationship between a spiritual guide, often very skilled, and someone well advanced on the Christian journey. But in this chapter I hope it will become clear that the work of spiritual direction at an appropriate level is something which many people can do and ought to be expected to take on as part of their ministry. It is certainly work which lay people ought to expect their ministers to be capable of. As well as the clergy, sponsors, friends, group leaders, catechists and other Christians who accept the responsibility of accompanying men and women on their journey into faith will also be engaged in a certain amount of spiritual direction.

The task sounds frightening because it seems to imply responsibility for someone else's soul. Certainly there should be training; there are things to learn and there are skills and attitudes to acquire. Some of them this section covers. Others can only be learned from other people, in dialogue and relationship. In some places there are courses available on Spiritual Direction for people with different experience ranging from beginners to fairly advanced practitioners. There are books, again varying in intensity. What there also needs to be is some kind of support, review and continuing development for people who are in this ministry. It is not for everyone, but it is for far more people than are at present engaged in it.

People are shy about matters of faith. They are reluctant to talk about spiritual experience and practice. You may well pray and your prayer may play an important part in your life but it is hard to be open about it. You feel it is private; perhaps you also feel it is inadequate, not good enough. This combination of not wanting to parade something which is intimate and not wanting to expose a weakness means that, while many people may be able to talk about their belief in God, they recoil from speaking about their friendship with him. It follows that they also feel chary about opening up the subject of how others pray.

For balanced growth into Christian maturity a developing friendship with God is essential; it is at the very centre of all that we are about. People usually need some help in cultivating that friendship. They need someone who will walk with them along their journey in this just as in the other aspects of their way to faith and commitment. This is the work of Spiritual Direction.

Praying

Prayer is the work of the Church, the Body of Christ. As the Christian community we, ordinary human men and women, are intimately caught up in the eternal relationship of love between Jesus and the Father in the Holy Spirit. This is what provides the basis for all our activity of praying. The worship which is part of the life of the Church comes first; it is one of the givens. During his lifetime the prayer of Jesus was the open offering of himself to the will of the Father. The Church's worship continues this prayer and is caught up in the eternal relationship of Father and Son in the Holy Spirit. Each Christian has their place and their part in it.

This theological belief about prayer finds practical expression in what goes on in the local church on a Sunday and in the wonderfully varied ways in which men and women give their attention to God either privately on their own or together with other people.

I want to stress the idea of variety. I am writing what I hope will help you if you are acting as a guide to someone on their spiritual journey. I also hope it may help you to reflect on your own journey, because that is needed before you can help anyone else. But your way of praying is probably different from theirs. Just as your face and figure and character are different. Once again it is vital to start where people are, not where you'd like them to be or imagine they are.

So it is useful when you are listening to someone to have some simple headings in your mind as a guide in discerning where they are and how, if at all, you can respond.

'Public' Prayer

I hinted to one pair of headings just now. You can sort prayer into 'Public' and 'Private'. Public Prayer is the common worship of the Church. Its form will depend on the type of Church. It happens when the community meets as the people who belong to Christ in that place to offer praise, thanks, penitence and prayer. Almost always they will follow a pattern, often a formal liturgy. Most often the common worship will be the Eucharist.

For some newcomers and enquirers and also for some established church members this joining in public worship may be their main, even their only way of praying. It stands rather like an oasis of refreshment in the week, when they can concentrate on their relationship with God.

Music is an important part of common prayer for a great many people. Hymns in Church are for many the only occasion for singing with other people. They engage emotions and memories in worship and are often the most meaningful part of a Church Service for certain people.

Common prayer is the prayer of the community. It has an ongoing quality about it, its own life and validity. I take part in it. I also take my part in it. That comes first. It may also be an occasion when I say my own prayers, bring my own needs to God and offer my own gratitude. But, in theory at least, this opportunity for private devotion comes second. The first thing about public liturgy is that it is corporate; it expresses the truth that Christians belong together in the Body of Christ.

'Private' Prayer

Praying on your own or with one or two other people is different from common worship. I want to spend most of this chapter discussing the ways in which people pray individually and how individuals vary. I have in mind the map on page 58 as a help in sorting out the different faculties and parts of ourselves that we bring into praying. It is not complete. You may well find it does not answer every situation, but I offer it and these notes as somewhere for you to start from.

People vary in prayer by the weight they give to these different aspects, which I have called 'Words and Systems', 'Thoughts', 'Images and Feelings' and 'Attitudes'.

Words and Systems

For some it is words that are the main vehicle of their praying. They like books of prayers written by other people to use as their own prayers; sometimes they write their own or make up their own set forms. Church services mean a lot to them, especially services with a fixed form and shape. They are people who like order and system in their relations with God. Daily prayers follow a pattern, perhaps for example working through 'A.C.T.S.' – adoration, confession, thanksgiving and supplication (asking) – or some other simple formula. Lists are helpful; lists of people to pray for, booklets of causes and institutions which ask for intercessions.

'Chatting with my friend God' is how one person described her prayer, going through the day and referring things to him which happen, decisions that have to be made, problems and worries encountered. For her and for a great many people prayer is a conversation, sometimes actually spoken aloud, more often voiced silently in the heart, with a God who cares

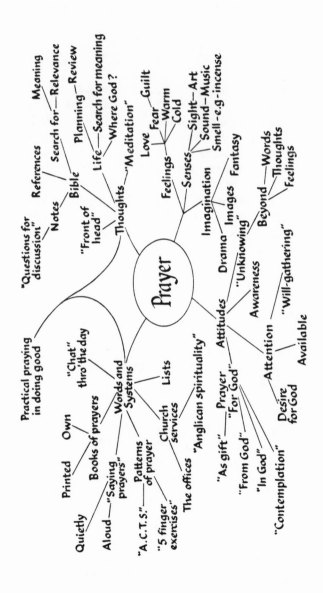

The Pattern of Prayer

and listens and from time to time is recognized as responding in some way.

Thoughts

Thinking about God, using the front of your mind to get in touch with him, to try to understand who he is or what he is about – that is how some people pray. For them the search for a meaning in life is about how to explain things, how to make sense. They are people whose intellect is important in their praying. For them the kind of Bible Study notes that are most helpful are the ones which end with 'questions for discussion'. They may find it easy and helpful to use a Bible with cross-references to other passages to compare what different writers have to say.

Faced with a problem, someone praying in this way may well think it through, worry it out with God in their prayers.

A friend of mine had been seriously ill. He could have died. He spoke to me afterwards about how he had been, as he said, unable to pray. He knew he was very seriously ill. He was facing the prospect of eternity and he found that he spent a great deal of time in his illness trying to think what eternity would mean and where God came into it. Normally, he was someone whose prayer was quite different, a mixture of set prayers and a feeling of warmth towards God. He found it hard to recognize that during his illness it was not that he had been unable to pray. He may not have been able to pray in the way he had before, but he was using another part of himself, his thinking mind, to pray with instead.

For another of my friends there are all the 'why' questions that spring out of the injustice and horror of famine and natural disasters. How is she to come to terms with a relationship with a loving God who is responsible for a created world where things like that happen?

Someone for whom this way of prayer is strongest is likely to find themselves more at home in a discussion group than in a prayer group. Their road to faith may well be along the way of

reason and argument rather than through music or dramatic
worship.

Images and Feelings

I was not sure whether to head this Section with the word
'Images' or the word 'Imagination'; because both are true of
another way people pray. It is not primarily using words, nor
is it using the thinking part of your mind. It is using perceptions and faculties which are, to use rather high words,
affective rather than intellectual. Praying in pictures, entering
into stories, living out dramas, carried by music, expressing
your relationship with God in song.

To return to the use of the Bible in praying: for people
praying in this way the Gospels are not a quarry for texts to
relate to other texts nor for evidence to support this or that
belief. The Gospels contain stories to be entered into. They
present people to be met in the imagination.

Prayer, the expressing of a relationship with God, has for
thousands of years been sung or prayed on a musical instrument. For someone who has appreciated Handel's 'Messiah' it
is almost impossible to read the Bible texts on which that
work is based without hearing the music to which they are set
echoing in the mind. I find that when in my prayers I want to
express praise to God it is often the tune of a well known
hymn of worship that means more than its words.

Imagination has to do with images, of course, but to use the
imagination in prayer is more than simply creating images. It
is letting the non-rational, non-intellectual side of your personality have its place in your journey into God. People spend
time happily fantasizing about all sorts of things, success at
work, sexual encounters, what to do if you win the Pools. Not
to mention the darker side of fantasy, the fears and distresses
which arise to scare and disturb you awake as well as dream-
ing. Fears of the death or injury of someone you love in an
accident. Even the simple fear of not putting the fire out when
you left home. Notice what happens inside you when you see

an ambulance answering an emergency call and are startled by the siren.

The prayer of images and imagination enters this area and opens this side of a person to God. Rather than thinking about incidents in life or incidents in the Gospels, the person praying this way enters into them in their imagination to experience their meaning.

Emotions play a large part in human life and they have their proper place in praying. For some people feelings are the heart of their prayer; for others just an aspect of it. Feelings of warmth or distance, of love or shame or the fear of the Lord of which the Bible speaks; being moved to prayer by anxiety about someone you love or by being afraid for yourself; enjoying a sense of comfort, reassurance and being in tune with God, which is how some people some of the time describe their praying. In these and many other ways the affective side of our nature is either a way into prayer, or a way of praying or a way of experiencing its affects.

Attitudes

Feelings can be a bridge leading into this fourth kind of prayer. Warmth, excitement, fear, anticipation, desire – all these focussed on God can be a way towards what I call the Prayer of Attitudes. In this you direct your whole self towards God in love or openness. This prayer of attitudes, though, is more than simply praying with feelings or with a feeling. It may have an emotional content, but what distinguishes it is that it is primarily a prayer of your attention; you may have arrived by way of conversation with God, by way of thinking or by way of imagination or feelings, but in this way of prayer you simply make yourself available to contemplate God as he is, open to be aware of him, waiting in his presence.

It is a way of prayer which, because of its nature, is very hard to describe in words. Even pictures are little help. The title of a mediaeval book about it, *The Cloud of Unknowing*, emphasises that it is not a prayer of the intellect. It is not a way in which there is much activity. You pray more by waiting, by being available. My image is of a she-cat hunting by long grass. She does not prowl dramatically about looking eager or menacing. She sits, at once alert and relaxed, and she listens. Her hunting consists largely of being aware of every sound in the long grass and discerning the distinct rustle made by a mouse or a vole.

This way of prayer more than any other illustrates what I believe to be the truest purpose of prayer. It is for God. This prayer of the will, of attitudes, points away from the person, their thoughts, feelings or concerns and dwells entirely on God as he is. God is recognisably both the source of the prayer and its aim.

The Body

People are not only souls or intelligence or feelings. We have bodies. Prayer is concerned with and affected by physical things in many different ways. Yoga has taught western men and women the importance of posture, exercise and breathing in a search for well-being and a balanced life. They are important aspects of Christian prayer too. Kneeling is one attitude for prayer and expresses humility. It is not the only way. Standing, sitting or lying are others. They each express something different about the relationship with God. Dance and movement can have their place in prayer either as a preparation or as a way of praying or as a form of response to God.

Spiritual Companionship

This very short survey of human spirituality is clearly only a rough guide. Libraries of books have been written about the subject and there are many living spiritual guides who can go deeper into it. However I feel it is important that it should appear in this book to give people accompanying others on their faith-journey an idea of the breadth of spiritual experience and of the resources for spirituality that lie in a human being.

I would expect anyone reading these brief classifications to recognise something of their own experience in several, perhaps all of them. I would also expect them to settle on one or two which most nearly fit their own present way of praying. All are perfectly right and valid ways of praying for any Christian. What is important is that a Christian friend can recognize and reinforce someone else in their growing friendship with God by helping them to develop on lines which are true for them. These lines may be quite other than the sponsor's own way of prayer. Spirituality varies. What suits one person may be quite improper for another.

When it comes to books of prayer or about prayer, be careful! You may have had it happen to you. A friend recommends a book, 'You must read it, it's marvellous. A lovely book.' When you try it, you find it dull, meaningless and not in the least helpful. It says nothing to you and you feel both guilty, because you've let your friend down, and also a failure because you are clearly not a good Christian if you can't enjoy and benefit from such a fine book. (The same thing happens with commending preachers and sermons.) Accept the truth that God has made people different and that he has given to each their own proper way to himself. Always remember that what is good for one may very well be no good for the next. Be prepared to pick and choose what suits you.

The work of accompanying demands a gift of discernment, an ability to listen and a certain degree of background knowledge. It requires both enough confidence and enough humility. The confidence comes from having accepted that it is part of the accompanying ministry to be a coach in spiritual matters and from having sufficient understanding of the basic principles of spirituality. It is also important to have proper backing and help from somebody else who is acting as your own guide. The humility comes from the recognition that the person you are accompanying has their own true spirituality and that your work is one of helping them under God's guiding to grow into what he has planned for them to become. The spiritual director is to be God's instrument, using their own gifts of perception, discernment and intelligence, certainly, but all for God and the other person.

John Westerhoff writes: 'The best guide on a spiritual journey is one who does not need to be helpful or needed, one who does not try to bear the responsibility for another life, but who can leave others in the hands of God – and get a good night's sleep. It is to take responsibility for one's own spiritual growth and be with others as they do likewise.'[1]

The Givenness of Prayer

Prayer is a dialogue. It is something which is a gift from God. He makes it possible for someone to pray. He is the inspiration. Without him there would be nothing. On the other hand prayer is a human work. It requires an effort on our part; it requires that we choose to put aside some time for it. We have to make ourselves available. We have continually to be recalling our wandering attention from all sorts of other thoughts, day-dreams and interests to the business of seeking God.

The most common danger at all stages along the road to prayer seems to be the danger of over-worrying and guilt at being a failure. Prayer is gift and our part in it is response to gift.

In the four-way analysis of prayer earlier in this chapter I was aware of a gap. The Charismatic Renewal sweeping through Churches of all denominations speaks strongly of prayer as gift from God, prayer as meeting a God who is spirit, who is the giver of life and relationship and power in prayer and in the human response to his call. This emphasis on the grace, the gift or, in religious technical language, the charism of praying should be recognized as a firm counterbalance to the common feeling that we need to work harder and harder to achieve and to succeed in spirituality.

Variations and Change

People who have prayed over a length of time, several months perhaps, several years certainly, will know that the temperature of their praying varies considerably. There are times when it feels warm and meaningful to pray; God is real and near. It is quite easy. However there are times when all that disappears. Praying is a cold, dull and lonely activity. It becomes difficult to persuade yourself that there is anything in it. God seems totally absent, if he exists at all.

Any spiritual director has to be aware of these variations. After all they are common enough to all praying Christians. Probably they are the source of most conversations about spirituality. 'I used to be able to pray. I used to enjoy it. But now I can't, it doesn't work any more for me.'

Putting it simply, probably far too simply, there are two possible reasons lying behind this experience of the emptiness of prayer and one which is commonly given but, I find, very often mistaken.

The reason which is usually false is the one which the person experiencing the emptiness is most likely to offer. It is that they are not trying hard enough; they think they ought to pray harder and they feel guilty about not doing so. This is a perfectly natural reaction but in my experience it is usually wrong. It falls into the danger of seeing prayer as only a human activity. It forgets the givenness.

What is far more likely is that the underlying cause is the regular dynamic of prayer. Like most human growth it develops in phases. Periods of brightness are followed by duller periods. There are alternately times of encouragement and help and times for developing our spiritual muscles. Dryness in prayer is a time for being faithful and staying with God; it is when the Christian learns to live by hope and faith and love for that which is not seen.

The skill of discernment and awareness of the spiritual director comes into play here, because the kind of boredom, guilt and anxiety someone feels in one of these times of dryness can also be a sign that the way they are trying to pray is in fact the wrong way for them. It may be that they have set out to follow a model which does not suit them or it may be that they have changed within themselves and are growing into a new way of prayer.

The four ways of praying I described earlier in this chapter can be different stages in one person's spiritual development. It is not uncommon to begin with simple prayer in words, using a defined pattern of prayer. Later you may find the system too tight and move to a more open, less wordy approach to God through the imagination or feelings or the will. The work of spiritual direction needs the sensitivity to notice the signs when someone ought to change and develop new ways of praying, or to support them as they come to terms with a time of dryness.

Practicalities

I am aware that what I have written so far will not be appropriate for everybody. To develop a pattern of prayer along the lines I have suggested may well be easier for people who can find the space for privacy in their lives and who are able to devote time in the day to it. It is not that you cannot pray unless you have leisure; rather it is that prayer has to be appropriate to the possibilities of life's demands.

For instance, the demands on a mother of a baby or small children or on someone caring for an invalid at home may well mean that prayer is a matter of a few scattered moments of turning attention to God rather than keeping a daily pattern of time offered as God's time.

Busy people and people whose life and work ask a lot from them may well see their prayer as offered in the things they do. It is a prayer of action, doing a job well for God's sake or consciously offering the care given to someone in need as a kind of intercession.

The Practice of the Presence of God is a short book by a lay brother in a monastery whose work was in the kitchens. In it he describes a way of prayer which is real to very many people whose lives are full of activity and little space. It is the way of carrying God with you all the time, working as if consciously in his presence, being aware of the spiritual within the every-day.

Pattern and Rhythm

I am someone who has been greatly helped by having what many Christians call a 'Rule of Life'. This is a way of describing the pattern of praying and other aspects of disci-pleship which are the basis of a person's spirituality. It could include how much time is given to prayer daily or weekly, the pattern of Bible reading and of Church worship, the propor-tion of money given away, time for family or for relaxation and other aspects of self-discipline which are appropriate. A rule of life like this is something to be worked out in discus-sion with someone else. The pattern should be sensible, possible to keep and not wildly beyond their ability! There is no point in setting such high standards that they can never be achieved. That just compounds feelings of guilt. Moreover there are people who feel strongly that for them what seems a rigid structure would reduce the spontaneity of their rela-tionship with God.

Praying with the Bible

The stories in the Bible are a central resource for someone who is trying to pray and to grow in prayer. But the Bible is a very hard volume for anyone to find their way round. Anyone who is acting as a spiritual friend to a new Christian needs to be able to guide them into a creative use of the scriptures. This means, first of all, selection. Short passages, incidents, stories and sayings are the best material to work on in prayer. Slow, repetitive reading to draw out meanings is often more valu-able than covering a lot of ground. So it is useful to have a system to select by. There are the Sunday readings; there are booklets of selections and notes published by the Bible Reading Fellowship, the Scripture Union and many other organizations. These cover a range of approaches to the Bible and are written for a range of different ages, abilities and interests.

Praying with other People

I began this section on praying with the central importance of the common prayer of the Church both theologically and as part of a Christian's personal spirituality. We need to meet with the community, to take our place in the prayers, the hearing of God's word read and taught, and to share in the breaking of bread in the Eucharist.

A different kind of praying with other people is group prayer. It is not the formal prayer of Church liturgy, nor is it private prayer taking place in company. It is important for people making their journey into faith to have some experience of it. In particular I suggest that groups accompanying people for baptism and confirmation should be sure to make time for prayer together. It should be more than a formal opening or closing with a prayer. There should be a space for perhaps a Bible passage, some comment, some sharing of ideas, reactions and concerns from people in the group; a time of silence and a time for open prayer, spoken or silent by the members.

Prayer groups are not without their dangers and may often need careful and experienced leadership. Before people can be open with each other before God there has to be a certain sense of confidence and a secure confidentiality within the group. But, given them, prayer groups offer their own particular dimension of praying, alongside the public worship of Church services and private prayer.

It can be a source of strength and fulfilment to join in prayer with one other person. Many married couples pray together as part of their pattern of family life.

5

Conversion

Central to all that this book is about and central to the work of accompanying people on a journey into the Christian faith is conversion. The word itself is a highly respectable, ancient Christian word. Maybe the way it is used in certain church circles has become so narrow that people from other church circles view it with suspicion. At its root, conversion is about turning, changing direction and this makes it a very suitable metaphor to use as part of the overall picture of a journey. So I intend to use it.

Before going any further, though, it would be as well to defuse some of the strange reactions some people have in the area of conversion. I trust that as you read on you will realize that I am talking about conversion in all sorts of different ways and over varying time scales. Certainly I shall notice the kind of experience which can be described as conversion in the narrow sense, often over a short length of time, accompanied by an onrush of fervour and emotion, but I am more broadly concerned with a great many different ways in which a man or a woman comes to a personal life-commitment to faith in and obedience to God as revealed in Jesus Christ.

New Testament Conversion

Different writers in the New Testament use their own pictures to describe the idea of conversion. Luke in the Acts of the Apostles has what for some people is the classic picture of Saul struck to the ground and blinded by the light on the road to Damascus, dramatically switched from persecutor to missionary preacher.

In Paul's own writings there is the image of pagans turning away from idols to serve the true and living God in 1 Thessalonians 1.9–10. He has the image of conversion as being altered into a new shape as in Romans 12.2 'Let God transform you inwardly by a complete change of your mind' (TEV). In 2 Corinthians 5.17 he has the lovely image, 'When anyone is joined to Christ, they are a new being; the old is gone, the new has come'.

However the most usual word, often translated 'repentance' or 'repent' is the one used by John the Baptist (Mark 1.4) and taken up by Jesus and his followers. It is about changing your mind or heart; being changed in the depths of your being.

Change is at the centre of the response evoked by hearing the Gospel. Some words and images are active; they indicate choices I have to make in order for change to come about. It is I who have to turn away from the old way to the new. Other words and images are passive; the changes happen to me as a result of my hearing the Gospel or of my being called into relationship with Jesus; I am reshaped and redirected. Both are true to human religious experience. In journey language there are corners and bends which are simply followed by the traveller and there are junctions and forks where the traveller has to make definite personal choices of the direction to go.

We often describe the start of this faith-journey as the expression of a need for an answer to questions about the meaning of life. This is not simply an intellectual question. It is about the shape and direction of mind and heart, about personality and purpose affecting the whole of life. It is to do with the inwardness of a person, how they see themselves, and with all their relationships, with other people, with things, with events, with the world around them and with God.

Terry was in his early thirties when his Mother and Father, taking their first-ever holiday abroad, were killed in a plane crash. 'I was shattered because I was close to my parents', he said. 'I couldn't make any sense of it. It seemed so unfair. I'd never had much time for religion or anything like that but I thought, "If anyone's supposed to have the answers, it ought to be the Church". So one Sunday I went to our local church. I'd never been in before and it was awful. Cold and dull and the Vicar's sermon made me think he'd never even asked any questions, let alone find any answers. But I didn't give up. I went to another church nearby the next Sunday and found it quite different. The people were friendly and welcomed me and the service felt alive. I went back for a few weeks and began to feel part of the place. I joined a housegroup. I had a long talk with the Vicar. It wasn't that I found answers to all my questions. I still don't know why it had to be Mum and Dad. I still think it's hard to have a God of love and all the suffering. The difference is I now reckon that there is a God like that and if he's like that then he knows the answer even if I don't. It all began to open out for me in the first few times in that friendly church. People there seemed to be concerned about me. They couldn't solve my problems but they didn't run away from them.'

Once it is recognized that conversion is all-embracing, it becomes clear that it cannot be a once-for-all happening. Conversion is a process. Certainly within that process there are likely to be high peak events – and also troughs and valleys. Bunyan's *Pilgrim's Progress* is only one of many classic portraits of the conversion journey, with his description of the long struggle to get to the goal. He pictures the dangers on the way from enemies on the road or the treacherous nature of the path itself and we are left with the strong impression that Christian at the end of his journey has achieved a maturity which has been won through life's encounters.

Certainly there will be for some people, but by no means for everyone, incidents, times and places, conversations or experiences which they remember as sharp turning points when they recognise that God can be seen to have acted decisively or which they know were moments when they made a definite choice for change.

In a world where the prevailing mood of people is increasingly non-religious, the process of conversion is often a lengthy and by no means easy one. People brought up and living in today's secular culture have attitudes very different from Christian values and often a deep ignorance of what Christianity is. The change which conversion involves is neither easy nor cheap. It may well be demanding. I hope that nothing I write will leave you with the idea that simply by following an offered formula you will be assured of success! It is not like that. We live in the world of real people and each one will follow their own route of conversion, or, it may be, of resistance to the changes which conversion initiates.

Points of Conversion

In describing different ways in which people come to conversion I have to offer a fairly arbitrary set of headings. There are many sorts of choices about change of direction in life, both active, chosen changes and passive, imposed changes. Different people will use different ways of analysing them and presenting them.

I find it simplest to use four headings. They are true to my experience of people and they are a handy guide to accompanying men and women on their journey. These headings work both when we look at how conversion comes about and also as we look at the changes which it results in.

They are the realm of feelings and emotions;

The realm of faith in the broad sense of attitude to life;

The realm of the intellect and understanding;

The realm of behaviour, how a person makes choices and decisions in their everyday living.

I have no desire to dissect human personality in such a way as to leave someone in different, separate heaps on slab. The whole tenor of this book is to say that people are whole and individual. My picture of the journey into Christian faith is of a journey which is towards coherence and a sense of being together. But experience shows that people's conversion and their routes to it are varied. Some people lead with their feelings, others with their spiritual search for purpose and meaning, others with their questions and arguments and others with the practical choices of living life. All these aspects are essential to what it means to be a human person. Genuine conversion, however much it may centre on one or other of these divisions, makes changes in them all.

It was the experience of giving her life to God at a Mission to London evening which led Maureen to our catechumenate group. She had been clearly moved by the music and by the speaker. She was in love with Jesus. However unbalanced some members of the group may have thought her reaction was, it was very clear that they all accepted the reality of her conversion. Over the weeks that followed they talked through its implications for her. There were strained relationships with two people at work which she felt badly about. She knew she had to apologize and do what she could to improve the situation. Prayer was a new country for her and she looked for help in developing it. Perhaps hardest for her was the need to come to terms with the very mixed nature of the church, that not everyone shared her experience and that in the parish congregation and even among the eight people who met every Tuesday in her group there were tensions and conflicts.

Conversion is both a continuous process, the process of being transformed by God and by conscious personal decisions into Christian maturity, and it is also a moment or series of moments at which sharp changes of direction can be recognized.

We are here dealing specifically with Christian conversion, about what happens when a person is taken by the Gospel, when God's story draws them into some participation or a degree of commitment. Or put it the other way, when a person takes God's story and makes it their own story, letting their life be moulded by what they perceive of God.

Evangelization is a word which can be used in two senses.

One, the sense usually found in Anglican circles, is the work of the evangelist, the missionary. It is proclaiming the Gospel where it has not been heard or accepted. The other sense is more to do with the Gospel having its effect upon someone. To be evangelized in this sense is not simply to be preached at, but to take hold of the good news of the Gospel or to be convinced and changed by it. It is a daily event and a life-long movement of change. Both the present, where we are now, and the future, what we may become, are important. They are the field for developing evangelization. There is a continuing tension between the two. We are forever faced with the challenge of turning from where we are now and turning to where we may go in the future. The Gospel is about hope and about movement.

Ancient Jewish prophets and New Testament writers spoke of turning from idols to the one true God, from the false to the real. Although there may not actually be idols on every British street corner, there are certainly plenty of idolatrous attitudes to be turned away from in contemporary life. The three temptations offered to Jesus in Luke 4 are still there for twentieth century men and women to turn away from in order to worship and serve the living God. Materialism, money and acquisition of things: – the power of Mammon is strong; appetites are there to be satisfied. Popularity, being admired, being successful are attractive. (How many advertisements play on the idolatrous worship of admiration?) Power, influence and prestige matter, both to those who wield them and to the powerless. Having power is a mark of the successful human being. To be powerless is to be a failure. Turning from these attitudes to Christian values is not easy. We live in an idolatrous culture. Faith, hope and love are principles which run counter to the prevailing direction. The transformation from self-centred to self-giving is a radical change.

Models of Conversion

As I have talked with people about the movement of conversion in their own lives and the changes which they recognize are connected with it, I have found there is a general trend towards a greater openness. It is not universal by any means, but as these people look back over their lives and as I look back over my own we find that with deepening commitment comes a deeper sense of freedom. There is less dependence on systems and regulations, less timidity, more willingness to change, more acceptance of being vulnerable to other people and giving room to ideas that are foreign. Trusting God leads to trusting generally. To be open to God means to be open to life.

In the section which follows I am aware of the danger of giving the impression that there is a hierarchy of importance, because one aspect heads the list and another only comes half-way down, or that there ought to be a progression from one to another for orderly development. No, it is a whole complex person and a whole complex of responses and relationships we are dealing with – all interconnected and all relating to and affecting each other.

Feelings

I put the emotional area first for two reasons. One is because I suspect that the majority of people come first to conversion through their feelings; it has many parallels with falling in love. The other is because of the important fact that we do not generally create emotions; we are affected by them: they happen to us. Dealing with feelings first is a kind of reminder that the initiative in conversion comes from outside a person's willing choice. It comes from God. The person's willing choice is in the nature of a response to God's stimulus.

Five minutes' walk away from where I live and work at St. Paul's Cathedral is Aldersgate Street. In May 1738 John Wesley had been to Evensong at the Cathedral and at a religious meeting in a house in Aldersgate later that evening he 'felt his heart strangely warmed'. From that occasion the whole direction of his life was changed.

Evangelistic mission preachers are well aware of the importance and power of the affective side of human nature.

Feelings of shame and guilt and the desire for love and acceptance provide a powerful stimulus for turning to the God who forgives.

Changes which take place in this area are changes from coldness to warmth, from being inhibited to openly expressing feelings, from fear to trust. It can be thought of as a change from resistance against God to a love for him and a desire to know and be close to him. Not that it all becomes plain sailing. Paradoxically one of the signs of deepening conversion is a sense of the need to deal continually with resistance, with excuses and 'good sensible reasons' for not going deeper.

It's an idea to work out for yourself the kind of characteristics, attitudes, feelings which you would look for in yourself or in someone else as signs of conversion to Christ. They may include a sense of gratitude, awareness of gift leading to expressing thanks to God. Or there may be a sense of the justice and truth or the majesty of God, a feeling of fear or awe, an awareness of guilt which is expressed in a confession of sins and repentance. Joy and pain may be there, sometimes at the same time. People may long to share their experiences by telling someone else or by engaging in some kind of practical action to make their world a better place.

Religious Faith

If conversion comes in and through the feelings for many people, it is the area of change in religious stance that is essential. I mean the change in attitudes to meaning, vision and purpose of life. James Dunning has described the basic movement in religious conversion as that from seeing life as a problem, as one damn thing after another, to seeing life as mystery, one gift after another, and responding with surprise and wonder. It is a movement to the recognition of grace and God as gracious.

For some people the movement is from religion in the head to religion as life. Patrick Purnell describes his youthful religion: 'You know the phrase 'religious dimension of life', meaning life divided into watertight compartments. Well, that in a nutshell is where the weakness lies. My religion was a dimension of life – a compartment of my life . . . I learnt that "God made me to know Him, love Him and serve Him in this world and be happy with Him for ever in the next'; that 'God is a Supreme Being who alone exists of Himself and is infinite in all perfections".

I could easily understand the need to go to Church to worship such a God, to make every effort to obey this God under whose all-seeing eye I spent every moment of my life, and the need I had to beg God's pardon when I broke one of the divine laws; and I was ready to accept that God would reward me for being good and punish me for being bad. All this I could understand: it was all so logical. What I could not grasp was how such a God could be part and parcel of my everyday life; I could not make this God part of my feeling life . . . In fact I wanted to keep this God at arm's length.'[1]

It is movement from believing *about* to believing *in*. For some it may come in a change from worrying about how Jesus did miracles to recognising the miracle which he works in them personally through giving them hope or joy or endurance. It may be the move from intense mathematical speculation about God as Holy Trinity to accepting that we live in and by the love of a God who gives to us our existence and who reconciles us, however rebellious we may be, with himself through Jesus our friend.

The Intellect

When I was dealing with ways of praying I made it clear that talking about the intellectual side of human nature does not necessarily imply that we are talking about what we loosely call intellectual people, academics, scholars and people who earn their living through their minds. We are talking about that ability which everyone has to work things out, to ask questions and to argue their way towards answers.

Some parts of the Church give very high value to the understanding. Faith can be seen as giving assent to statements about God. For people whose way to conversion is through the mind the actual step which marks conversion is more often than not one which is not rational or logical. The willingness to change is often shown by the willingness to take not an ordered step but a leap in the dark. It is to jump over from one set of mental attitudes, one system for ordering life without God as a factor in it, into a different system which relies on God existing, creating and redeeming. Conversion in this sense can be described as my coming to make sense of my life only if God is part of that sense. Among the many living images in St. John's Gospel is that of Jesus bringing truth to people and 'the truth shall make you free'.

The danger for the intellectual is that things of the mind can simply stay in the mind. The way of conversion is for thought about God and Jesus, analysis and acceptance of religious statements, to change into an acceptance of this truth which is God as the one central meaning of life.

Tony Bridge, formerly Dean of Guildford, has described his journey from an atheism which was his reaction as a young man to the distorted Christianity offered to him as a boy. Through study of philosophy he came to see 'that it was much more rational to believe in God than not to believe. There was far better reason in the end to believe that there's some kind of ultimate spirit, reality . . . but the mere fact that that was so, didn't make me believe at all. Which shows how really limited the intellect is. I find it fascinating, but it didn't make me believe. All this process came to a head when I woke up one summer morning and discovered to my absolute horror that something had happened in my head, so to speak. There'd been a slight shift of angle of viewpoint and I knew that I believed something. So I came to believe that there must be some kind of ultimate spirit beyond, just to make sense of anything, including myself and you and everyone else.'[2]

Behaviour

So conversion is about changes which come through and are effective in someone's emotions; it is about a radical shift in their deep personal attitude to life's meaning and purpose and it concerns the way they think and find answers to the questions life puts to them. The way these changes show is in the things they do and say. How a person lives is a sign of the values that motivate them.

Sometimes these may be sharp, clear changes demanded by the Gospel. It is part of some preachers' stock-in-trade to have a repertoire of loose living, drug taking, dishonest, worldly people who were claimed by Christ and are now reformed characters. But most people seem to live without that sort of high drama. 'Conversion of morals' is often a slow business of questioning the way I live and trying to measure it against the way of Christ as I see it. It is the difficult business of recognizing how much the way I live is simply a reflection of the way people around me live. I pick up my sense of right and wrong from my family and friends. Standards of honesty, the importance of solidarity with other people, the importance of independence and achievement can all vary according to my social class. There are grey areas, for instance, between what is accepted as 'middle class morality' and what is Christian morality.

Rarely is it possible to look to the New Testament for specific answers to moral questions. Our society and our world are so different from the first century. What we can look for is principles upon which to base our own decisions. St. Paul's conversion from living by Law to living in response to God's grace can find a parallel in the way for many people the movement of conversion is away from a dependence on rules or the external pressures of their own society towards accepting a responsibility for themselves and for their own choices and decisions as they come to give more value to the principles of self-giving love and of the infinite worth of the other person.

Conversion and Church

Two other dimensions of conversion need mentioning before I turn to think of the ministry of accompanying people in their conversion. The first of these is conversion in relationship to the institution of the Church, discovery of the living reality of Christ present in his body, to put it in rather high blown theological words.

For people who have had some relationship with Church, people who, while not necessarily claiming membership, would say they went to services, the movement is from formality to a living faith. Such men and women are likely to accept the attitudes of the community. They recognize that their adherence to the Church implies some agreement with its beliefs. But their faith is 'of the Church' rather than deeply, consciously their own. For them the movement is towards personalizing faith, expressing their individual awareness of God and their own commitment. It is to take consciously for themselves the living centre of the community's belief in the move from formal to experienced relationship with God.

There is a mirror image to this. For people who come to faith from a non-church background, whose journey began in the world of secular culture and belief, it is often the attraction of Jesus and the friendship of a few Christians which supports and encourages them. Their conversion may be strongly through their feelings or their intellect and have little sense of the wider church. There is a sense in which they need also 'conversion to the church'; recognizing that relationship with God implies relationship with brothers and sisters in his community.

I am aware that that sounds very fine, but I can hear, if not protests, at least anxieties about the kind of church I am expecting people to be converted to. Once I accept that it is important that the Christian finds his or her place in the church, I am faced with questions about whether they are likely, as I said just now, to find 'the living reality of Christ present in his body'. The need to accept, welcome and accompany new Christians should force the members of the local church to ask searching questions about their community life. Is it something worth converting to?

The World and the Kingdom of God

Turning from the inward outwards does not stop with developing a full life as a Christian within the community of the church. Jesus did not come to found a club for friends but to herald the Kingdom of God. The church is commissioned to forward his work, to proclaim the Good News of Jesus and to be an agent of that Kingdom in our own generation. As a community and as individuals Christians are to work for God's will to be achieved in the lives of individuals, societies and nations. God transforms us as we answer his call to conversion not so that we may feel better but so that we may accept his work of mission.

Conversion to mission involves a man or a woman in the same way as it involves the church community in a three-fold work of evangelism, being a witness to the Gospel; of service to the needs of others whether that is personal help of individuals or working on and through the structures of society; and of building up the church with the support and continuing formation which that calls for.

'Stewardship' is a current cult word but I believe it is closely linked with this aspect of conversion to the world. Stewardship is a perception of our own place in the world and our responsibility to and for people and things in the world. It is a change from an attitude of ownership, from domination and exploitation to one of management, service and loving respect.

Within Stewardship, of course, comes the proper use of money. One aspect of conversion is the conversion of the pocket. This can be a very hard area for attitudes to change.

Accompanying Conversion

Conversion, as we have seen, is a movement of change in which both the person and God are active. It also involves other people. In this section I want to offer some ideas to help people to recognise and be sensitive to what may be happening with those they are accompanying. I remind you that this is not a how-to-do it manual and that everyone is different.

You will know from your own experience how much the movement of conversion owes to the intervention of other people in your life. You might find it helpful to stop reading for a moment and just make a list of those who have helped you to where you at present stand in your own journey of faith.

You may well remember something a friend said which met a particular need at the time. It could be the example of a known Christian's behaviour at work; the warmth of welcome at a mother and toddler group, or the words of a powerful preacher.

I have found and there is plenty of evidence from other people that in the way men and women come to conversion there is usually someone in the church or in the Christian group who acts as a link, a bridge of welcome and friendship. Quite often it may be a fiancé, a husband or wife or a close friend or relative, through whom somebody is introduced to the life of a Christian community. Sometimes there is simply a welcoming person to greet a newcomer. In any case the role which a sponsor plays is vital. Support and encouragement are also part of the work done by a group of people. I have many vivid memories of the powerful help given by leaders and members to one another in the often difficult searching and discovery of meaning and purpose in the hard situations in which life had put them.

Delicacy is needed to avoid the danger of indoctrination, over-pressuring. The relationship of the enquirer or the new Christian with sponsor or catechist or the welcoming group which accompanies them is ideally one where the friendship and support provides help but allows freedom. It is adult Christian maturity which is the goal, not slavish conformity. People have to be respected and to be given the full right to choose. They have to follow their own way to God, not some pattern predetermined by the tradition of the particular

Church or the personal experience and vision of the individuals who accompany them.

Above all the key words which mark this work are sensitivity and discernment. Another person's conversion is not forwarded by giving a great deal of information, even less by full instructions on how to do it. What is needed is a willingness to engage in clear and open dialogue in which the other is enabled to listen to God and to make their own decisions.

For this ministry to be fruitful there needs to be an environment of trust and acceptance. My experience has been that the groups of established church people and newcomers provide this. Obviously there is the need to watch the effect of the group processes. The ideal balance is to provide for the atmosphere of loving, tolerant support for each person to grow without the love turning to demand or the toleration breaking into anarchy. In the first there is a danger that people will be forced at a pace or in a direction which is wrong for them, in the second people can be badly hurt if their confidences and their openness are abused or betrayed.

A final reminder as I close this section. The ministry of a sponsor or a catechist is one which demands courtesy. It is the person you are helping who matters. The journey and the changes, the discoveries and the blockages all take time. Sometimes there will be moments of hope, excitement even. Sometimes there will be periods of struggle and difficulty. This first stage in the Christian pilgrimage is only a beginning. The rest of life lies ahead as the time for growth and further discovery of the meaning of what it means to be a disciple. Conversion is not only an initial turning. It is a continued and continual awareness of our need to be changed more and more into the likeness of Christ. There may be occasional glimpses of what it means to achieve a small step but always there is the future hope of true fulfilment.

6

The Church Community and the World Community

If the journey into Christian faith is to be complete it needs to include initiation into the Christian community by Baptism or Confirmation. It cannot be a lone journey ending simply in a deeper personal self-awareness. Other people are involved. So is the whole apparatus of the Church with its systems and its relationships. But the movement is two-way: it is not enough to see how the newcomer is to be introduced into the fold. The presence of the newcomer with all that he or she brings with them is in itself a challenge to and a change in the community. We need to look both at the effect on the new Christian's journey of the fact of the Church and at the effect of the new Christian's joining on the Church he or she joins.

The Church somebody joins is an actual group of people. It consists of a core of dedicated people with leaders and helpers; there are the regular worshippers who make up the committed membership and there is an outer fringe of adherents, well wishers, nominal members and friends. For many of the people about whom this book is written the journey will be from the outer edge of the Church into the more dedicated centre. That move is one external aspect of their conversion.

To enter more deeply into the life of the Church means getting used to the ways of the Church. Partly this is a matter simply of becoming at home in the community but partly, I would hope, it is a matter of testing for oneself the values and relevance of those ways.

There is plenty to learn and plenty to test. Sponsors and

catechists need to be aware of how new and strange many of
the Church things they have taken for granted will seem to a
newcomer. Churches have their own smell. There is the
attitude of respect for the past, for tradition, for what has
been inherited, whether this is a set of doctrinal statements or
a decaying piece of embroidery. There are rituals to be
learned, whether these are the events of liturgical worship or
the importance of jumble sales, beetle drives and Friday
evenings in the Social Club. There are special languages to be
learned, again both in worship and in the business and
fellowship life of the Church. There are some attitudes which
are generally recognized as acceptable in each particular
community, some which are seen to be open to debate and
others which are excluded.

The question of Church disunity has to be faced squarely.
Although the journey into Christian faith is a journey into
relationship with God, the journey of conversion, it is also
one which is accompanied by Christians of a particular
denomination and issues in the sacraments of initiation as
practised by a particular denomination in a particular local
fellowship within one broken Church.

The scandal of the divisions within the Church is one of the
challenges brought by new Christians to the Church as they
find it. There are, of course, many others. If we look at the
story of the Church as told to an enquirer we find it a mixed
one. There are high points, glories even. There are also times,
incidents and attitudes of which as members we are ashamed.
Having to retell them faces the Christians accompanying a
newcomer with need to come to terms with the history of
their own Church and with the present state of it. Doing this
may well urge them towards a commitment to working for
change to put things right in their Church where they can.

At different points in this book I have mentioned things
about the local Church which either help or hinder people in
their search for God. At the risk of repetition I want to bring
some of them together here.

Unity and disunity between Christians and between churches

are continuing features of church life. A local church where you can sense the warm quality of friendship and unity is attractive. Spitefulness and self-seeking repel. It matters how a Christian community deals with disputes and friction between people and groups. Newcomers will soon notice if there are cliques or mistrust. I have in mind the parable of Christian love given by a church hall kitchen with shelves of locked boxes, each containing the private tea cups of a different church organisation!

I keep stressing welcome, because it matters. It needs to be as unconditional as possible. There is a real danger of churches degenerating into clubs with a closed membership for people of a similar sort and this needs to be faced honestly. How much part does social class play in the life of St. Jude's? Do you have to fit in before you can be welcome? Flexibility comes into this too. With every new member who joins something alters because they bring in a new element. If a community is strongly traditionalist, this can be felt as a threat. 'We don't want new people changing things in our church.' It is fine if someone is looking for the security which that set kind of attitude can offer and is willing to accept its rules. But for the encouragement of the journey of discovery you need a community which is more open to experiment and willing to be changed and developed.

The process is one of dialogue. Two partners are involved and each is open to giving and receiving. Both are likely to be changed. In the small accompanying group this is most obvious, because each member there affects and is affected by the others. The same thing happens with the wider congregation. I have seen churches in which the working of the catechumenate has brought a new life and vision, with a strongly increased sense that lay Christians have their own valid ministry in the worship, the mission and the service of the local community. The Rite of Christian Initiation of Adults celebrated publicly enacts the deepening stages of the enquirers' commitment. Simply by their presence and by the involvement of the congregation in their journey the people who are coming to faith and the sacraments of initiation influence the life of the church they are joining and challenge people in it to look to their own commitment and understanding of faith.

Wider Vision

I am vividly aware of the danger which faces Christians, in England at any rate, of treating their church as a refuge from the hardships and difficulties of the world. It is a temptation which is very attractive to clergymen and congregations are often happy to follow them into a kind of ghetto. In the way I have structured this book I can see that I have let myself be seduced into a collusion with the people who expect a book about the Christian journey to be mainly about life in the Church.

But the Church cannot be seen in isolation from the world, just as no person can be isolated from other people or from society. It is not possible to live simply for yourself or by yourself. The Church was founded to be for the world and to work for God's rule in the world. It can only be true to its nature if it is open in its mission to the world within which it lives.

The trouble is that in most churches the available energy is devoted to maintaining the structure, whether this means repairing the buildings or propping up the organization. The effect is that the task of equipping Christians to be agents for mission in their own milieu does not come high on the list of priorities. Yet it is an integral part of anyone's journey in faith that they arrive at an understanding, at values and attitudes which give shape to their relationship with and their place in society and in their world. The local church's task is to enable this to happen.

I see a real danger of the initiation of adults into church membership stopping dead just at that point. Men and women are not encouraged to move onwards to engagement as Christians with the world in which they live. Of course it is more comfortable to stay within the walls of the church and to limit Christian commitment to things of churchy interest. But it is a sad travesty of conversion.

Mission is many-sided. Conversion to Christ carries with it involvement in his mission. Both for the individual and for the church community I see it as three main interlocking activities.

Evangelism is the presentation of good news to other people whether this is by word of mouth in conversation or from a pulpit of some kind in public proclamation. Personal and community witness are an essential part of it. How people live and how groups behave sometimes give as forceful a testimony as actual words.

Service of the needs of others is the practical side of mission. To feed the hungry, bring health to the sick and liberation to the oppressed are only a few instances of it. They call for both time and effort from men and women and involve political and social action both from individuals and the community.

Body-building is the development of the skills and gifts of the mature member of the Body of Christ as well as of the community itself. Mission here involves prayer and training and education.

The issues which have to be considered are not easy because the claims of the Kingdom of God often run counter to what each of us would prefer. There is also the scale of issues, which easily leaves people baffled. Peace and justice are ways of identifying that Shalom, the rightness of things with God, which is part of what we mean by the Kingdom. But does the idea of peace and justice stop at where I can do something about it? I can make up the quarrel with my neighbour about the broken fence; I can speak up at a Union branch meeting and support someone against unfair treatment; I can use my vote as carefully as I can in the Council or Parliamentary Elections. But what about world peace, America and Russia, the arms race and the North-South divide between the rich and the poor nations?

Even on the intimate, personal scale of events, relationships and choices where an individual is involved and can see some effect from how they act, it is often hard to see what bearing Christian faith has on the way things are. At one level I have heard the problem presented clearly by a financier in the City of London, 'I am a rich man and I am a Christian. I read the parable about the judgement of the sheep and the goats on whether or not people have helped those in need.

'As a wealthy person who is a Christian, I do my best to give generously in support of the needs of other people. What is very much harder is to see how I, as a Christian in a senior position in my firm, can make sure that our business decisions are influenced by the same principles.'

In another area of work I recognize the cost to a man in a factory trying to stand out against the racial discrimination against black workers and sexual harrassment of women coming on to the floor which are part and parcel of the place.

The story of the development of Industrial Mission in Britain and Western Europe provides a parable which has a bearing on this conversion to the world. Since World War II there have been three phases. In the first the church in the shape of its ministers recognized that while it exercised some ministry to families at home, men at work were missed out. Industrial Chaplains and missioners therefore visited factories to meet and 'pastor' those who worked in them.

It became obvious that it was not possible to 'pastor' or evangelize individuals without some reference to the conditions in which they worked. Industrial Mission developed from being mission simply to people at work to being also mission to the structures within which they worked, seeking to understand the way firms and industries behaved and how they were organised and to look at them from the Christian standpoint.

The third phase is the present position where it is recognised that industry is part of the wider society, subject to the forces of world economics and having effects upon all parts of human community. Industrial Mission is involved in bringing

Christian insights to bear on such things as the multinational companies, unemployment, and inner urban decay.

Faced with the world and its life, I find it sad when the 'Time and Talents' aspects of a Christian stewardship programme seems to limit offerings to those given for the service of the church, when a plumber is encouraged to see his Christian commitment as largely fulfilled by maintaining the church heating system rather than in the way in which he does his weekday work on a building site; or when a bank worker is snapped up as a church treasurer rather than encouraged in his idea of standing for election as a local councillor.

None of this is easy. Nor are there any generally accepted guidelines, let alone any correct answers. What I hope that the process I am talking about provides is the means to encourage and equip people for their ministry as lay men and women living out their faith in the world in which they have their work and their homes and their leisure interests. I hope too that the kind of groups I describe will be a forum in which they will be enabled to explore the meaning and the practical expression of that ministry with other people for whom it is a real issue.

7

Equipped for Ministry

It is not possible to write a manual for the ministry of accompanying someone else into faith. In this chapter I can simply point to the equipment people need for this work – the skills, the knowledge and the attitudes. But they have to set about acquiring that equipment themselves. All through this book I have described the process of the formation of new Christians as being one of dialogue. It is about relating with others and in groups. The same is true of the formation of men and women in the ministries of sponsors or catechists. You cannot learn it from a book. You need to learn from experience, by practice and by reflection on that practice.

In what I suggest as ways in which church communities and their leaders can work together to develop these ministries, I bring together much that has already appeared in earlier chapters. It is in no sense a blueprint to be followed slavishly. The right model for any church to adopt is one which grows naturally out of the life of that church and which makes sense to the people who are active in it. Although there should be elements which are common to all, the way one church follows will almost certainly vary from that used by a neighbouring church.

The first of the common elements in the training of leaders is that everyone who exercises a ministry in the accompaniment of others into faith should have their own personal experience of speaking and listening openly about their life and faith. This includes the clergy. It calls for the kind of environment in which priest and lay leaders can be honest together and accompany one another's journey. Each has gifts to offer and each needs to be respected. There is no way in which the professional ordained minister can be thought of as having concluded their journey. Priests, deacons and members of religious communities travel the same road as the newest enquirer. Certainly they may have travelled farther, acquired more knowledge and skills, but they still have to do exactly the same personal work of growing in awareness of God and in the light of his love reviewing their own lives. It is all too easy for the professional to say 'The Church teaches that God is . . .'. What is far more demanding is to say, 'For *me* God is . . .'. Many people who hold authority within the Church find this difficult, because their own personal faith seems far less well formed and less sharply defined than the teaching they have come to accept as Church doctrine.

Group Training Example

Let me suggest some ideas for a session with people who are starting in this sort of ministry. There will be several men and women in a group, say between six and ten, perhaps fewer. The purpose is to help them reflect on God's purpose for them through reflecting on their lives and the gospel in company with others.

The first phase is to talk about what is important at the moment to each of the people in the group; working in twos or threes is suitable here. It involves talking about something that really matters. It also involves the hearers in listening as well as they can. What is happening is that people are putting into words part of their own life-story and their companions are giving their attention, entering into the experience of someone else.

The second phase moves from concentrating on the story offered to looking at the Christian story, some aspect of the Church's inheritance which has some bearing on it. It may be a Bible passage, it may be something about church life or a personal experience of the Christian life. Narrative is likely to be more useful than doctrine. People need to be helped to engage with different faculties, their feelings, sympathies and imagination as well as with their intellect. Story-telling does this better than exposition of dogma.

In the third phase the stories are brought together in conversation within the group. Life and Gospel meet and each person is asked to see what consequences follow from that dialogue. What does it mean in these particular circumstances to say, 'I am a Christian'? Where do I go from here?

In this book I envisage the main work of Christian formation taking place in small groups, rarely more than eight or ten, often in pairs, threes or fours. There is a need to recognize each journey as individual and personal. It is something intimate which needs to be respected. I suggest that the formation of leaders should show the same characteristics. If we hope that catechists and sponsors will be good listeners and be able to discern sensitively, then these skills are to be developed in their formation and in the support and review which is part of their continuing in-service training.

Leading groups is in itself a skill which needs to be developed and the principles and practice of how to help groups and group members should be part of the preparation and support of catechists.

It will be clear that what I have in mind is a team, perhaps only a small one, in which priest and lay people work openly together, each exercising their own vital and distinct ministry. There is a mixture of relationships; there is the relationship of colleagues sharing in an enterprise and there is the relationship of leader and led, helper and helped. Let it be recognised very clearly that it is not always the priest who is the leader or the helper! Often, of course, that will be so. There is the responsibility the priest has as the pastor of the flock, the responsibility as the one charged to guard and hand on the tradition of the church and the responsibility of presiding in worship. But these responsibilities do not prevent the priest from accepting help or guidance from other people.

The Church of England report *All are Called* warns of the danger of the 'Shepherd/Sheep Syndrome' by which a priest hardly ever learns even from very committed lay people and lay people retreat into a superficially respectful but resigned or cynical attitude to their 'Father in God'.[1]

Theology

For many people theology is a frightening word. They think it means being able to recite the whole of Christian doctrine. No, theology is an activity in which people take part. It is the work of men and women thinking about God and his relationship to themselves and their world. Seen in this sense, virtually the whole of this book is theology. There is a proper lay theology which is exemplified in the work I describe. I do not want to deny the value of academic theology. The Church's tradition of belief and scholarship needs to be continually reviewed and its presentation renewed in each generation and for each change in circumstances. Indeed the kind of lay theology I mean can only work if there is a living tradition of thought and study of the Christian inheritance in universities, colleges and schools.

There must be some element of education in the formation of catechists and sponsors. If they are to be able to tell the Gospel story and to represent the church tradition, they have got to know enough about them to handle them honestly and effectively. For many established church people this knowledge will have come over the years of membership. They will have acquired a familiarity with Bible stories and ideas from church services, from sermons and from their own Bible reading. They will be familiar with the pattern of the Church's year and the Creed it pictures. They may well have given time to Lent Courses, Parish Weekends and Retreats. Many districts have study programmes in Christian subjects leading to qualifications in some kind of lay ministry. Some of these will be predominantly educational and concerned with the content of belief and study of it. Others may include training in the skills of ministry.

What I would hope from any programme in the area of lay

theological education would be that it should give to people
engaged in it firstly the opportunity to acquire knowledge of
the Christian tradition, its content and the documents it uses;
then some facility in the use of those resources and in making
judgements about them and, thirdly – for me essentially – the
ability and the interest to think theologically about matters of
importance in life. By this third I mean that I hope people will
be enabled to relate the first and second parts of their education to the events and choices of real life. I have a horror of
students being left with an enclosed capsule of religious
knowledge which does not connect with anything outside its
own narrow historical, biblical or ecclesiastical field.

Fears

I recognise that much of this book will cause people to feel
afraid. There is the lay person's fear that he or she is inadequate to undertake the responsibilities I suggest they should
accept; they feel they do not know enough; they are not good
enough; they see themselves as less than the fully committed,
praying Christians they imagine are really needed to do the
job. To which I answer. 'Fine. O.K. That may be true, but
who else is there? And if you don't start from where you are,
you'll never start at all'. Accepting responsibility for a ministry, exercising a ministry and growing in competence as a
minister all go hand-in-hand.

The fear is a natural one and has to be met by providing the
kind of formation I have outlined and also by the provision of
really adequate team support and on-going formation all the
time.

I recognise two clerical fears. One is the fear that the new
Christians, the enquirers, will be taught less than adequately.
The question I am asked goes something like, 'How can you
be sure your confirmation candidates have been properly
instructed if you don't do it yourself?' I hope that if you have
read through my book as far as this, you will have some idea
of my answer to that one. It is that while I recognise the

questioner's anxiety, I am less concerned to see that the whole dogmatic syllabus is covered than to know the person has moved to that point along the journey of conversion where they can truly say, 'Jesus is Lord'. It is not essential for me as a priest to accompany that journey. Often indeed having a priest as the companion only complicates matters.

The other fear is a personal one. It is about loss of status and purpose, a fear that the priest's responsibility will be diminished if lay people take over some of the pastor's teaching role. I meet it by showing how there is a rather different ministry to be found, one which is both more demanding and more exciting. The priest is the one who supports, informs and leads the ministry of the people who make up the Church in the place.

Wolfgang Bartholomäus writes, 'In the long run, self-determined Christians will only feel at home in communities which promote mutual self-determination ... Self-determining communities live, not exclusively, yet in part from the inspiring power of the priest.'[2]

The Church is not priests: it is the whole people of God, only a handful of whom are deacons or priests or bishops. There is a genuine professional joy to be found in helping others to discover and develop their vocation as mature Christians in ministry to others.

Speaking for myself I have found that this helping and leading the church in the place to fulfil its ministry is a more valid expression of priesthood than simply doing the job myself. On the other hand I recognise the danger that it is often quicker and less trouble to do just that – to try to do it all myself. In that way less and less gets done and the priest becomes increasingly more tired and less effective.

8

Resources

There is a considerable body of experience and understanding of the Adult Catechumenate for individuals and churches to draw on. It is to be found both in books and periodicals and also in the meetings, training events and contacts offered by different networks and groupings. All are there to be used. If you want to find out more, please make use of them.

Networks

Roman Catholic

The North American Forum on the Catechumenate offers comprehensive training institutes for different levels of experience in the catechumenate, publishes a newsletter and is a mail order book seller. Address: 5510 Columbia Pike, Suite 310, Arlington, VA 22204, (703) 671-0330.

Episcopal

The Evangelism Ministries Office of the Episcopal Church Center conducted a pilot project in the Diocese of Milwaukee. The project, "Living Our Baptismal Covenant," sought to apply the catechumenal process to adults entering congregations through baptism, reaffirmation, reception or confirmation. Information and resources are available from Rev. A. Wayne Schwab, Episcopal Church Center, 815 Second Ave., New York, NY 10017, (800) 334-7626.

Associated Parishes is an unofficial network of Episco-
palians and other Christians interested in liturgical renewal. Resources are available on the theology and practice
of Christian baptism. Membership is $20.00 per year. Con-
tact Co-ordinator, Associated Parishes, 3606 Mt. Vernon
Ave., Alexandria, VA 22305, (703) 548-6611.

Association of Diocescan Liturgy and Music Commis-
sions. Contact Rev. Clay Morris, St. Mark's Episcopal
Church, 600 Colorado Ave., Palo Alto, CA 94306, (415)
326-3800.

Lutheran

The Academy for Evangelists is a national network for
the promotion of evangelization and Christian initiation.
Contact Rev. James M. Capers or Rev. Paul H. Pallmeyer
for a listing of members or further information. Address:
Evangelical Lutheran Church in America, 8765 West Hig-
gins Rd. Chicago, IL 60631-4188, (800) NET-ELCA.

Official Texts

The Rite of Christian Initiation of Adults, 1988. This edition
of the rite was mandated for use in the Roman Catholic
dioceses of the U.S. as of September 1, 1988. It contains all
of the various rites for the catechumenate, the sacraments
of initiation, and the post-baptismal period of mystagogy.
It is available from the U.S. Catholic Conference and from
a number of other publishers.

The Book of Occasional Services (The Church Hymnal Cor-
poration, New York, 1979). This contains an official Anglican Rite of Christian Initiation of Adults produced by the
Episcopal Church's Standing Liturgical Commission.

Books

Becoming Adult, Becoming Christian, James Fowler (New York: Harper and Row, 1985). A study of adult human development and the stages of growth in faith.

Breaking Open the Word of God, Karen Hinman Powell and Joseph P. Sinwell (Mahwah, NJ: Paulist Press, 1986, 1987, 1988). A three volume set of resources for using the Lectionary in catechesis.

Building God's People, John Westerhoff III (Seabury: New York, 1983). A detailed and compelling account of the work of catechesis, covering all aspects of the Christian life.

Celebrating Our Faith, Robert E. Webber (San Francisco: Harper and Row, 1986). An introduction of the catechumenate tradition to the Protestant Church showing how adaptable it can be to all denominations as a means of contemporary evangelism.

Conversion and Community, Thomas P. Ivory (Mahwah, NJ: Paulist Press, 1988). Explores how the catechumenate can serve as a model for total parish formation.

Conversion and the Catechumenate, ed. Robert Duggan (Mahwah, NJ: Paulist Press, 1984). A full, practical treatment of conversion and the ministry of accompanying new Christians.

How To Form a Catechumenate Team, Karen Hinman Powell (Chicago: Liturgy Training Publications, 1986). A guide for pastors, catechists, sponsors, welcomers, and catechumenate directors.

The RCIA: Transforming the Church, Thomas Morris (Mahwah, NJ: Paulist Press, 1989). A complete guide for the pastoral implementation of the rite.

Stories of Faith, John Shea (Chicago: The Thomas More Press, 1980). A full development of the use of stories in the growth of faith and the sharing of faith.

Welcoming the New Catholic and *Guide for Sponsors,* Ronald Lewinski (Chicago: Liturgy Training Publications, revised

1987). Two short, very practical handbooks for use by clergy and lay teams in the parish.

Journals and Newsletters

Catechumenate. A Journal of Christian Initiation. Published bimonthly by Liturgy Training Publications, 1800 North Hermitage Avenue, Chicago, IL 60622.

Catholic Evangelization in the United States of America. Published bimonthly by the Paulist National Catholic Evangelization Association, 3031 Fourth Street, N.E., Washington, D.C. 20017.

Forum. Monthly newsletter published by the North American Forum on the Catechumenate, 5510 Columbia Pike, Suite 310, Arlington, VA 22204.

Fire and Water. A quarterly newsletter for the catechumenate published at St. James Episcopal Church, P.O. Box 4463, Jackson, MS 39216, (601) 982-4880. $15.00 per year.

Notes

Chapter 1

1   *Rite of Christian Initiation of Adults*, Geoffrey Chapman, a division of Cassell Publishers Ltd., London, 1987, p.5. Copyright ICEL.

Chapter 2

1   John Shea, *Stories of Faith*, Thomas Moore Press, Chicago, 1980, p.43.

Chapter 3

1   Norbert Mette, *The Christian Community's Task in the Process of Religious Education*. Concilium 174. *The Transmission of the Faith to the Next Generation*. T. & T. Clark Ltd. Edinburgh, 1984. p.73.
2   John Westerhoff III, *A Pilgrim People*, Seabury Press, Minneapolis, 1984, p.1.
3   Karen Hinman Powell, *Beginnings Institute* Conference Papers, North American Forum on the Catechumenate, 1986.

Chapter 4

1   John Westerhoff III, *Building God's People*, Seabury Press, New York, 1983, p.117.

Chapter 5

1 A. Patrick Purnell, S.J., *Our Faith Story*, Collins, London, 1985, p.28.
2 Tony Bridge, *Road to Damascus*, Thames TV Broadcast, 1986.

Chapter 7

1 *All are Called*, Church House, Publishing, London, 1986. p.8.
2 Wolfgang Bartholomäus, *Being a Christian in the Church and the World of Tomorrow* Concilium 174 *The Transmission of the Faith to the Next Generation*, T. (T. Clark Ltd., Edinburgh, 1984. p.83.